BAD MEN, NAUGHTY BOYS

This book challenges the socially accepted constructions of male dominance and the destructive, aggressive behaviours of men, encouraged during childhood and into adult life. In doing so, it highlights the resulting damage and destruction inflicted upon society, boys, men and others. The volume disputes the concept of an "ideal man" promoted by adults and the media, which normalises and encourages disruptive, aggressive behaviours and risk-taking activities among boys during childhood and throughout adulthood.

The book continues to further highlight the negative consequences of such masculine behavioural norms upon our society and questions the society's widespread complicity in encouraging and normalising the harms such behaviours pose and inflict. Examining issues such as prison population, knife crime and boys' exclusion from school, it explores the damage such behavioural norms inflict upon boys and young men, as well as how their actions, shaped by these norms, ripple through the wider society. As well as examining relative data and academic literature, this book includes the narratives of school staff and excluded boys, which illustrate how adults and boys in schools hold hegemonic masculine ideals as valuable.

This book is designed for both academics and non-academics and will be useful to students and researchers in the fields of psychology, gender studies, sociology, social work, community and public mental health. It will also appeal to professionals, counsellors, life skills trainers and general readers.

Jack Banner has worked with boys and teenagers for over 40 years as a teacher, headteacher and college lecturer. All his academic work has centred around studying and understanding boys and the reasons for their problematic behaviours in schools and society. He has written theses for both an M.A. and an Ed.D. on this subject.

BAD MEN, NAUGHTY BOYS

Challenging Accepted Male Behaviours

Jack Banner

Routledge
Taylor & Francis Group
LONDON AND NEW YORK

Designed cover image: AlexLinch via Getty Images

First published 2026
by Routledge
4 Park Square, Milton Park, Abingdon, Oxon OX14 4RN

and by Routledge
605 Third Avenue, New York, NY 10158

Routledge is an imprint of the Taylor & Francis Group, an informa business

British Library Cataloguing-in-Publication Data
A catalogue record for this book is available from the British Library

ISBN: 978-1-041-22535-5 (hbk)
ISBN: 978-1-041-22538-6 (pbk)
ISBN: 978-1-003-73278-5 (ebk)

DOI: 10.4324/9781003732785

Typeset in Sabon
by Apex CoVantage, LLC

To Linda, for your support, encouragement and love

CONTENTS

AUTHOR'S NOTE

In the media, there is regularly a great deal of discussion and debate about boys' behaviour in schools, knife crime, road accidents, misogyny and so on. Although ideas to address these problematic issues are regularly proposed, none consider or explain them in the way that I am suggesting. I explore the root causes of this issue and, within this, debate about how it might be resolved.

My book begins by questioning why we ignore the huge amount of damage that men inflict upon the world and what might be done about it. I highlight the problems that male behaviour has upon our society and question why we ignore and encourage the huge amount of harm that masculine behaviours have upon our world. I examine issues such as prison population, knife crime and boys' exclusion from school. I argue that society broadly normalises and naturalises these problem behaviours and in doing so encourages and condones them, deeming them desirable. The pressures upon boys in schools to conform to particular forms of masculinity come from fellow pupils, school staff and parents.

I argue that male dominance in society has for many years relied upon male aggression over those unwilling or unable to conform to particular forms of masculinity. This has resulted in the acceptance, normalisation and promotion of such behaviour, even though there is little evidence that it is either normal, useful or constructive.

Dr Jack Banner

INTRODUCTION

An alien visitor unaccustomed to our world might be forgiven for thinking that there is something very odd about the male species of the human race and that our world might be better off without them. After all, compared with women, men are responsible for the majority of crimes, extreme violence, including wars, the majority of murders, domestic abuse, aggression, thefts, riots, road accidents and football hooliganism – the list is exhausting. While an alien visitor might wonder why we accept and even encourage such behaviours, strangely, society in general appears to be unconcerned. Through a study of academic literature, verifiable data and interviews with boys and practitioners, this book explores the contradictory constructions of masculinity and deviancy held by society. It explains the damage being done and the reasons why it appears to be unchallenged; it also discusses how practices in schools contribute towards exacerbating this issue, and finally, it discusses how this matter might be alleviated.

While this book discusses at length the issue of problematic masculine behaviours in our society, it also explores constructions of masculinity in schools and the problematic behaviours of some boys. This is because there are very strong links between boys' problematic behaviours in schools and the subsequent destructive behaviour of men. This is shown through an examination of discursive accounts provided by teenage boys, all of whom had been excluded from school, and the accounts of educational practitioners working with such boys. Boys' disruptive behaviour and educational failure are significant social justice issues because permanent school exclusion is directly related to deviancy, unemployment and crime.

While much of the information, evidence and data for this book are drawn from the United Kingdom, it can be shown that this issue is a

DOI: 10.4324/9781003732785-1

worldwide problem and, as such, is comparable and universally relevant and through out.

Of particular importance is that boys' behaviour and peer interactions are very similar throughout the world. The book shows that peer pressure among boys significantly contributes towards perpetuating and normalising particular myths about masculine behaviour, aggression, risk-taking and male domination over females and alternative masculinities. The book also shows how some boys, through drawing on discourses of patriarchal and hegemonic masculinity and gender binary asymmetries, construct themselves in ways that contribute towards school confrontation. These disruptions are shown through class disruption, aggression, peer interactions, risk-taking and subject choices. The voices of practitioners show how they also contribute towards tensions, how they also perpetuate misconceptions and how education policy is considered as prohibiting staff from working effectively with some boys.

This book exposes the challenges that boys and practitioners face as they negotiate the dominant masculine discourses at large in both school and home. It also shows that respondents' understandings of masculinity rely on outmoded discourses of masculinity, essentialist gender binaries and constructions of childhood, which contribute towards problem behaviours in school. Tensions in school are also exacerbated by policy discourse and practitioners' constructions of childhood. However, while these normative discourses are challenged by respondents' acknowledgement of alternative versions of masculinity and the coexistence of gender heteroglossia, the book shows how damaging dominant masculine behaviours remain powerful in schools and wider society.

Consideration is given to literature discussing the social construction of parenting, childhood and children's "needs". Literature regarding the persistence of the role model discourse as both a cause and solution to boys' problem behaviours in school is also investigated. Literature examining hegemonic, problematic masculinities is used to further understand how it is performed and enforced through peer interaction, resulting in problematic behaviours, which dominate particular constructions of masculinity.

The theoretical framework used for this book draws on the work of Foucault (1970, 1977, 1980), who theorised that people construct truth through the dominant discourses, which they draw on. I also consider the work of Ivan Jablonka (2019), who discusses the history of masculinity and explains why dominant, patriarchal masculinity has acquired and maintains such importance in Western society. This book uses the work of these authors to explain how and why power is afforded to one discourse at the expense of another, and thus, why damaging patriarchal discourses are so prevalent. Of significance is the research undertaken involving narrative interviews, using discourse analysis as discussed by Gee (2011) and Taylor (2001). The information and data collected from these interviews are contrasted with the literature to further understand how schools contribute towards validating and thus perpetuating the myth that is masculine superiority.

1

NORMALISING BAD MEN'S BEHAVIOUR

"A mans gotta do, what man's gotta do"

While many of us might rarely question the behaviour of men and boys, as mentioned, an alien visitor might be forgiven for concluding that there is something not only different about men compared to women but also something very odd about their behaviours, behaviours which lead to so much destruction, and yet society seems accepting of this harm by normalising it. So, let us begin by exploring some of the problems that men and boys are said to be responsible for.

The prison population

While a school pupil might be relieved that certain misbehaving boys are removed from their classrooms, as a man, you ought, however, to be very concerned about prison statistics. Yearly records (which remain consistent from one year to the next) show that there are approximately 84,000 people in prison in England and Wales, with men representing 95% of this prison population (http://www.prisonreformtrust.org.uk 2015). These percentages are much the same throughout the Western world. What these statistics suggest is that there is something very seriously wrong with some men compared to women. While courts, when sentencing, might be more lenient on women than men, this does not account for the disproportionately high number of men incarcerated. Consequentially, it might appear logical that because there are so few women in prison, men must be naturally more deviant than women. Men thieve, embezzle, vandalise, rob, stalk, fight, maim, kill and

DOI: 10.4324/9781003732785-2

kidnap; the list of crimes that lead to a prison sentence is immense. And it is not surprising that reports show that men have always dominated the prison population, year in and year out, persistently and considerably outnumbering women in prison (Berman 2009). But it needs to be noted that incarnation is not unique to adult men. Under-18-year-olds who commit crimes are confined, with under-15-year-olds in secure children's homes, 12–17-year-olds in secure training centres and 15–18-year-olds in young offender institutions. The majority of those confined, thus, are male.

Although some people are concerned about the large numbers of people in prison and the conditions they are subjected to, the fact that men have always represented such a huge proportion of the prison population appears to be unquestioned. As a result, this historical perspective contributes towards the acceptance and normalisation of these statistics and, as a result, the lack of action to investigate this matter further.

Similarly to school exclusion, while you might be glad that disruptive boys are removed from classrooms, you may also be quite content that thugs, thieves and murderers are also removed from our streets. We know that aggression and violence significantly contribute towards schoolboy exclusion, but why are we so unconcerned about so much male deviance?

It is blatantly clear that particular male behaviours are very problematic. It could therefore be argued that if men behaved more like women, there would be fewer difficulties in schools, there might perhaps be less crime, there would be fewer men in prison, and our schools, towns and cities might be safer. In relation to this, ex-Prime Minister Boris Johnson suggested that Russian President Putin would not have ordered the war against Ukraine if he were a woman (Tapsfield 2022). He also argued that Putin's masculine behaviours were toxic. While this simplistic view ignores the complex politics and economics involved in the attempted Russian invasion of Ukraine, there are some issues of similarity.

Statistics relating to school exclusion and prisons illustrate troubling acts of male deviance, aggression and violence that overwhelmingly outnumber those of girls and women. Generally, politicians and the media appear to show little concern about these staggeringly apposing statistics specifically relating to men. At times, there have been calls for strong, masculine men to work in schools to "control" problem boys (Cushman 2008; TDA 2008; Gove 2011; McGrath and Sinclair 2013). Although this may appear a logical and sensible solution, it has also been argued that such a strategy would prove to be counterproductive because it would not only potentially reinforce the idealism of the effectiveness of male strength and aggression but also do little to address the issue as to why male strength, aggression and violence are considered, by many, to be natural, normal and desirable attributes for men. Desirable, that is, until such behaviour intrudes and becomes problematic. Domestic abuse is one such intrusion.

Domestic violence and abuse

While not ignoring or condoning those women who abuse children and/or their partners, it is nonetheless men who significantly dominate domestic abuse statistics. Men's physical abuse of women considerably outnumbers the smaller statistics of women's violence towards men. This is somewhat illustrated by the large number of women's refuge centres secreted around the country. It has been argued that abuse is a way for one person to control another. While this may sometimes be so, it does not fully account for all the physical and mental abuse that takes place each day. Some men, it appears, use their partners and children not only as a means to dominate but also as a means to vent their frustration and anger. This is shown by the rise in such behaviour during some sporting activities. As an example, in England, statistics show that during the 2014 World Cup, domestic abuse, perpetrated by men, increased by 38% whenever England lost a match (BBC.co.uk 2018). Anecdotal evidence also shows that during the 2018 World Cup, domestic abuse continued to be an issue, increasing in frequency during and after England matches. Prior to the 2024 Euro football tournament, news reports warned about the possible increase in domestic violence related to the success or otherwise of Scotland and England matches (Baines 2024). However, it has to be emphasised that domestic abuse does not end when the football season is over.

Male use of dominance, aggression and violence is not limited to the frustration of watching sport. There was also much concern over the spike in domestic abuse throughout the COVID-19 lockdown period. Towards the end of March 2020, the UK government told the country that people "must" stay at home and that certain businesses must close. This was a particularly difficult time for many people, and sadly, it saw a huge increase in cases of domestic abuse directly related to the isolation and confinement caused by the "Stay At Home" order. Statistics published by the Office for National Statistics reveal that between April and June 2020, there was a 65% increase in calls to the National Domestic Abuse Helpline (Havard 2021). Unsurprisingly, men perpetrated the majority of these cases of abuse.

While female groups rightly campaign about domestic abuse and seek help for female and child victims, the question of why men do this and why men are generally more aggressive and violent than women appears to be little asked. This question, therefore, remains unanswered but will be explored and debated further later.

Murder

Men are also murderers, and regretfully, domestic abuse does sometimes result in murder. As one might expect, data on homicides show that, of the

551 murders recorded in the United Kingdom in 2012–2013, it was men who dominated these crimes (ONS 2014). Men commit 90% of murders. In addition, 75% of murder victims are men. So, when a murder occurs, the victim and the perpetrator are overwhelmingly likely to be male, not female. Notably, such statistics are similar throughout Western society. In addition, female victims of murder are more likely than men to have been killed by a partner (a further possible link to domestic abuse), while men are more likely to be killed by an acquaintance than a stranger. These differences do not appear to have any relationship with genetic or biological differences but do have a direct link to violent and aggressive male behaviours, behaviours that it seems our society is content to accept. This will also be explored further later on.

However, murder is not unique to adult men. Males under the age of 18 have committed murder in the past and have been executed for doing so (Stern 2025).

This is reflected in statistics for knife crime in the United Kingdom, which has over the last few years escalated in prevalence and therefore has attracted a great deal of attention from the media. Once again, boys and men dominate the statistics relating to the use of and being the victim of this weapon. In 2008, the BBC reported that one in five teenagers carried a knife (BBC 2008). This has increased significantly since then, as has the number of knife murders (Allen and Audickas 2018). Knives are used for sexual assault, for intimidation and for murder. Knife crime is more prevalent in areas of poverty, where crime is involved and where there is gang violence (Coid 2021). Not surprisingly, the majority of knife crimes were committed by young men, but shockingly, 21% of these crimes were committed by boys under 17 years old, and the number of knife crimes is continuing to grow. In 2017, there were almost 35000 recorded knife crimes, with knives being used for robbery, intimidation, sexual assault and the wounding and murder of other men (Allen and Audickas 2018). However, it has to be acknowledged that fatal stabbings of teenagers are particularly high (Benkinsella.org.uk 2025). The BBC, drawing on information from the Office of National Statistics, reports that in 2023–2024, there were 64 fatal stabbings involving those aged between 13 and 19 years. It is clear that murder is not unique to older men.

The aggression of men towards men is particularly pertinent because one of the features of many under-achieving and disruptive schoolboys is their commitment to male strength and aggression, particularly towards other boys. Academics argue that in schools, violence by males against males is often interpreted by school staff as "boys being boys" (Mills 2001). As already discussed, such an attitude has the potential to legitimise, condone and normalise schoolboy violence. Worryingly, normalising such schoolboy violence mirrors societal attitudes towards male violence and, it appears, the apparent reluctant acceptance of it.

Risk-taking

Linked with aggression and the "boys being boys" attitude is the notion that boys and men are somehow naturally more boisterous and adventurous than women. Indeed, a generally perceived feature of masculine behaviour is the acceptance and expectation that boys and young men will engage in risk-taking activities. All school pupils will have witnessed boys mucking about and doing dangerous and risky things: balancing on walls, throwing stones and performing stunts on bikes and skateboards. Academics argue that boys engage in such activities in order to demonstrate to others that they are tough and unquestionably masculine, not feminine (Ludden 2020). Some believe that girls are incapable of engaging in such activities, and if they do, they are often considered odd (Halberstam 1998). Nevertheless, as a result of boys' engagement in risky activities, statistics show that boys and young men are far more likely to have accidents, sustain injuries and attend A&E than girls of a similar age.

In relation to this, a European Transport Safety Council publication attempted to understand if gender had a part to play in road safety. The publication shows that in 2011, men accounted for 76% of road deaths. It also drew on research which showed that men were more likely to engage in dangerous and risky driving activities than were women (ETSC 2015). These figures are furthered by a UK Department of Transport report (2012; Parliament 2023), which indicates that in the United Kingdom, male drivers account for 80% of young persons' accidents. A 2020 report further corroborates these facts, stating that men are more likely than women to kill someone while driving a motor vehicle and ten times more likely to do so while riding a motorcycle (Allen 2020). It seems clear that the male desire to engage in risk-taking activities is directly related to traffic accidents involving men and, as a result, has a profound impact on deaths and injuries on our roads. Insurance companies recognise that young male drivers are more dangerous than young female drivers but are forbidden from differentiating insurance premiums based on gender. While as a society we are generally concerned about road safety, we do not, however, appear to be doing very much to address the issue of the reckless driving activities of men.

Recently, in France, because of the large number of road accidents and fatalities involving male drivers, a campaign has been started to encourage men to drop their macho driving image, and they are being urged to "drive like a woman" (Anon 2024). Although statistics illustrate that female drivers have fewer accidents than men, it is debatable if such an advertising campaign will have any influence on those men who use driving as a means of proving their masculinity. This is because for those men who draw upon a dominant male discourse and appose being compared and contrasted to females, such a campaign might encourage them to demonstrate more vigorously those tough and risk-taking characteristics that they consider so important to them.

So far, all the statistics presented have related to boys' and men's problematic behaviours. It is these behaviours that I argue require examination. It seems that demonstrating one's masculine skills of strength, dominance, aggression and violence is of immense significance to many men and boys.

Misogyny

While the emphasis of this book is not about femininity or female equality, it is essential to acknowledge that misogyny, which is the male domination and subjugation of women, is a further example of the unpleasant, damaging and unnecessary characteristics of some men. It features in many of the problematic male behaviours discussed earlier.

Misogyny is the ingrained prejudice or hatred towards women. It manifests in various ways, from overt acts of discrimination and violence to subtle, everyday behaviours that devalue women and their contributions. Such misogynistic behaviours range from blatant aggression to concealed actions that undermine women. These behaviours include the use of derogatory language, objectification, dismissing women's opinions, victim-blaming and controlling behaviour. Such practice of masculine prejudice against females is rife throughout society, religion (Alba 2019) and schools (Government 2023). It is carried out by those men and boys who believe that men are superior to women, and it maintains the dominant social position of men over women. As Simone de Beauvoir and Ivan Jablonka explain, misogyny reinforces and maintains patriarchy and has been widely practised throughout the world for thousands of years, as can be seen in historical events, politics, art and literature (de Beauvoir 1949; Jablonka 2019).

A further indication of this has been shown in recent years with persistent accusations of misogyny in political parties (Parker 2023), the police force (Manning 2023), the fire service and some professional sports (Shemilt 2023). The UK government, in its attempts to tackle this issue, has published guidance to schools (DfE 2025; GOV.UK 2025). While this action might be applauded by some, the guidance does little more than instruct schools to deal with the undesirable behaviour of some pupils. The guidance does not consider or tackle the reasons or causes of misogyny in schools.

It is my opinion that the subjugation of women will persist until the issue of problematic male behaviours and the pressure on men and boys to conform to such behaviours are fully addressed. Patriarchy, as Ford and Allen argue, is used to legitimise and reinforce misogyny (Ford 2019; Allen 2025) and in itself remains an issue in schools and society.

The terms "adult" and "child" are so commonly used that there seems little purpose to question what we mean by them. However, having discussed the problems of aggression and crime, it is clear that while adult men dominate these acts of hegemony, teenagers and young boys are also guilty. We may therefore wish to differentiate between what is understood as an adult man and what is considered a child, a boy. Such differentiation between boys and adult men is tenuous at best.

Childhood is an ambiguous area. Academics such as Cannella (1997) and James and James (2004) argue that childhood is a social construction, formed within cultural discourses but also shaped by government policy. Over the years, the idea of what constitutes a child or an adult has changed significantly. It is said that childhood was invented in the nineteenth century when school was made compulsory; before then, children went to work, as did their parents. They were not considered as children but as small versions of adults (Cannella 1997). In the 1800s, when compulsory schooling was first introduced, the school leaving age was ten. It was eventually raised to 12 until, in 1944, the earliest age at which pupils could leave school and go to work was 15 years (Jones 2003a). It was then raised in 1971 to 16 because of the rising number of unemployed youths. Currently, in the United Kingdom, schooling is compulsory until 18; thus, it appears that our understanding of what it means to be an adult or child appears to be directly linked to the currently enforced school leaving age.

It is then clear that hegemonic masculine behaviours are not unique to older men but coexist in men and boys at all ages. What is of particular significance is what happens in and at school and then how this impacts boys'/men's behaviour into adult life.

2

CONSIDERING NAUGHTY BOYS' BEHAVIOUR

> "What are little boys made of?
> Snips, snails and puppy-dogs' tails
> That's what little boys are made of"
> (nineteenth-century nursery rhyme)

Disruptive and deviant behaviours

Boys and girls attending school will be aware that a number of pupils get thrown out of school because of their uncooperative, aggressive and disruptive poor behaviour. Each year, the figures are consistent; some 8,000 pupils are excluded from schools across England and Wales. However, of particular significance is that, of the hundreds of pupils temporarily and permanently excluded each year, boys represent the highest proportion, being four to five times more likely to be excluded than girls. UK government statistics, released yearly, show that verbal and physical aggression and violence towards fellow pupils and teachers are prolific disruptive issues in schools (DfEd 2018). It is therefore of little wonder that those who engage in such disruptive behaviour in school risk being thrown out. Regardless of various government initiatives and interventions, these figures remain stubbornly consistent from one year to the next.

Presumably, some school pupils may be relieved that such boys are removed from their classrooms; after all, their behaviour has the potential to disrupt lessons and their learning. Interestingly, while government ministers, parents and teachers occasionally indicate some concern about the large numbers

DOI: 10.4324/9781003732785-3

excluded, little attention appears to be given to the fact that the vast majority of those thrown out of school are boys. Girls only make up a small percentage. As the principal reason for exclusion is boys' aggression and violence, it would be useful to try to understand such behaviours, particularly if we wish this issue to ever be resolved.

And that is an important point. Does society consider it an issue requiring attention and needing resolution? How often have you heard the expression "Boys will be boys" in response to a boy's misdemeanours? As Clementine Ford argues:

> When people chuckle and dismiss bullying and aggression as a simple case of "boys being boys", they're . . . maintaining a particularly one-dimensional idea of laddish masculinity.
>
> *(Ford 2019, p. 18)*

I would suggest that such comments legitimise the acceptance and normalisation of particular boys' behaviours, such as aggression, risk-taking and boisterousness, all of which contribute towards classroom disruption and boys' exclusion from school. And it has to be added and also contributes to accidents, injuries and deaths involving boys and young men. This will be discussed further in a moment.

It might also be argued that certain boys' poor behaviour and the accompanying disengagement and educational under-achievement are major gender and social inequalities, which need to be explored, thoroughly understood and resolved. Although some academics have and continue to investigate this issue, it appears that at a government level, these issues are hardly being considered at all. While statistics in relation to boys' behaviour and exclusion are collected, it seems that they are then both accepted and ignored by those encumbered with the responsibility of overseeing our education system. This is particularly disquieting, as statistics indicate that those who fail at school are more likely to become involved in crime and go to prison (Berman 2009). And as Millham tells us, this has been the case for many years (Millham et al. 1975).

Exclusion from school

Teachers and many young men at school will be only too aware of those boys whose daily activities surround deviance, aggression, showing off and mucking about behaviours, many of which relate to those discussed earlier. You will also be aware that poor behaviour at school often results in many of these young men being temporarily or permanently excluded.

As already stated, government data indicate that boys were some four times more likely to be excluded from school than were girls. I now suggest

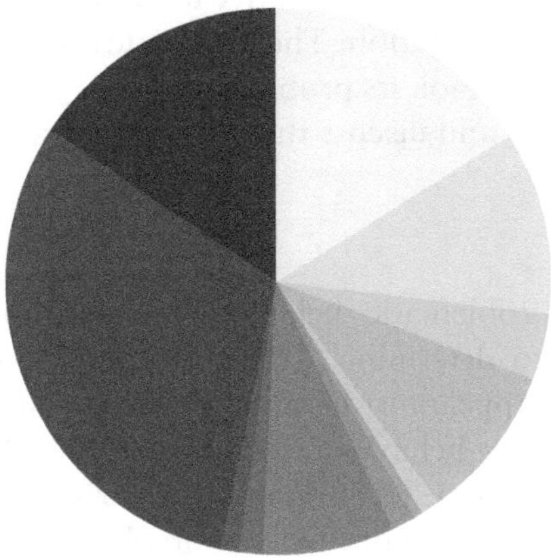

FIGURE 2.1 Reasons for permanent exclusions.

that boys' dominance of exclusion statistics correlates with the statistics for domestic abuse, crime, prison population, risk-taking and traffic accidents as discussed earlier. Further to this, when one examines the reasons for boys' exclusion from school, the relationship between excluded schoolboys' behaviours and problematic adult behaviours is startlingly similar.

The pie chart above, taken from UK government statistics (DfE 2014b), shows the range of behaviours which result in boys' exclusion from school. In doing so, it highlights the wide range of threats and acts of physical violence which dominate the problematic behaviour of excluded boys.

The statistics for school exclusion remain fairly consistent. As an example, in 2017–2018, there were approximately 4,000 permanent exclusions from schools in England. In addition, there were over 400,000 temporary exclusions (DfE 2019). These figures ought to be disturbing, but there is little indication that society cares, with insufficient effective government intervention and interestingly limited media acknowledgement. It is frankly unsurprising to learn that the majority of those excluded were boys, not girls. However, in ignoring this fact and accepting that this is just "boys being boys", we are potentially condemning many boys to a life of chaos and poverty.

We know that boys who do not attend school are at risk of becoming involved in crime. So it would appear to make sense to try and keep such boys in school, and there has been a government initiative to do so. However, as I will show, this is a far too simplistic solution. The leaning towards crime is not simply a result of not attending school. Its problematic roots go further and in another direction. I shall clarify and discuss this in greater detail later.

Hegemonic masculinity

Having considered the range of problematic behaviours perpetrated by men and boys, it seems necessary to determine a suitable label for them. The term "hegemonic masculinity" appears to be an appropriate and suitable label for the disturbing masculine behaviour discussed earlier. It was coined by Raewyn Connell in 1995 (Connell 1995) and has, for some time, been used to describe such problematic masculine behaviours. Haywood and Mac-an-Ghaill (2003) describe hegemonic masculine behaviours as the domination of one group over others through subordination, agreement or marginalisation. While agreeing to the latter, Connell and others have recently revisited this issue, arguing that there are a multitude of masculinities, with violent masculinities and hegemonic masculinity being at the top. (R.W. Connell and Messerschmidt 2005) They explain:

> Hegemonic masculinity was understood as the pattern of practices (i.e.: things done, not just a set of role expectations or an identity) that allowed men's dominance over women to continue. Hegemonic masculinity was distinguished from other masculinities especially subordinate masculinities.
>
> *(Connell and Messerschmidt 2005, p. 832)*

Louisa Allen, discussing the concept of hegemonic masculinity as a "type", argues that hegemonic masculinity is a position within a range of masculinities and that alternative masculinities are subordinate. She also adds that hegemonic masculinity encapsulates the idea of the "cultural ideal" of masculinity, which is popularised by society (Allen 2025). This concept is particularly relevant, as I shall discuss later.

It appears that one label to describe problematic masculine behaviours is insufficient. Throughout this book, it will be necessary to use other terms to discuss and describe these issues, such as patriarchy, dominant masculinity and toxic masculinity. Therefore, I shall use a range of descriptive labels, some of which have subtle but important contextual meanings.

In schools, as I shall discuss later, boys are unaware of the labels attributed to these problematic behaviours. As I will show, what boys are doing is submitting to and then copying certain behaviours in order to be seen as a "real" man or, as Mills discusses, "an ideal man" (Mills 2001). While having a name or label seems important, I would pose two further questions. Firstly, I continue to ask, why, as a society, do we accept and foster the current status quo of dominant, destructive masculine behaviours? Secondly, while we debate the name to give to these problematic masculine behaviours, should we not also be considering what name we should give to the man who does not follow, copy or foster hegemonic masculinity? What that descriptive name might be remains a mystery.

3

MICHEL FOUCAULT

The core of this book involves attempting to understand how boys at school and school staff working with them accept, criticise and understand constructions of masculinity.

Exploiting Foucault's lens allows for a critical exploration of how people normalise and attribute truths in their understanding of men's and boys' behaviours. Of particular significance is considering how people draw on certain "discourses" to "construct" boys' and men's behaviours.

Discourse

It is first necessary to understand what Foucault meant by the term "discourse". Although the word "discourse" may be understood and used in a variety of ways, Foucault acknowledged that his definitions of discourse,

> "do not conform with current usage: linguist usually give the word discourse a quite different meaning". He then added, "the term discourse can be defined as the group of statements that belong to a single system of formation".
>
> *(Foucault 1972, p. 121)*

Importantly, discourse integrates what we say and also what we do. Foucault discusses different forms of discourse, such as clinical discourse, economic discourse, and the discourse of natural history. Elaborating on this, Kendall and Wickham (1999) say that discourses are productive and give examples: "medical discourses . . . produce the mentally ill, penological discourses

DOI: 10.4324/9781003732785-4

produce the criminal, discourse on sex produce sexuality" (Kendall and Wickham 1999, p. 34).

Foucault explains that these examples of discourse have an author or authors.

However, and of particular importance, in an earlier work, Foucault also discusses those discourses where the author cannot be determined. He said:

> there exist all around us plenty of discourses which circulate without deriving their meaning or their efficacy from an author to whom they could be attributed.
>
> *(Foucault 1970, p. 58)*

This comment is of particular importance when looking at the views and constructions of interviewees who make claims about the "normality" of certain behaviours without having evidence to support their beliefs. Discussing this, Foucault explained that it is within such a range of discourses that people construct "knowledge" and ultimately "truths", and all members of a society are implicated in preserving specific discourses. This is because we, both knowingly and unknowingly, use and exploit unproven, indistinct cultural and historical rules and behaviours to support certain discourses, thus effectively affording the discourse power and knowledge.

Various authors have discussed discourse. For example, Hewitt defined discourse as:

> Broadly speaking, the . . . characteristic ways of conceiving, speaking and writing about things. . . . Such texts always conceal an ideology, a set of beliefs that are not based on any empirical evidence, but only on the interests and preferences of those who hold them.
>
> *(Hewitt 1976, p. 27)*

Discourse is then understood to be the limiting and accepted ways of discussing and referring to things. Reinforcing Foucault's description of discourse, Prado (2000) reiterates that while discourse is an integrated set of things we say, it also includes things that we do. This suggests that discourse is not only about the culturally permitted ways in which we are allowed to speak about things but also about the customary and normalised ways in which we are to act in particular circumstances.

Other authors also make reference to particular types of discourse, examples being policy media and common discourse. Ball (2008), for example, makes reference to "policy discourse", which may originate from schools but also stems from government educational policies, which he suggests make some ideas "true" and thus influence teachers' and staff attitudes and beliefs in schools. Macdonald (2003) discusses media discourses and refers to forms of publishing, including television, radio and newspapers, suggesting the "notion of the media reflecting reality" (Macdonald 2003, p. 12). The influences of the media upon male beliefs will also be discussed later. While Garfinkel (2003) refers to common discourses, referring to the established, accepted and normalised manner of discussions and casual utterances. What Garfinkel explains here is that there is a range of discourses, deriving from official and unofficial sources, which people draw upon as truth to engage in a range of conversations, with the understanding that those engaged with them will understand, agree and accept the normalisation of the utterances.

For this study, the discourses operating in schools are of particular interest. In schools, we might, for example, consider the manner in which pupils and teachers interact. The language used and the physical interactions between pupils and teachers are constructed by both government and school policy discourses and influenced by media and common discourses. Operating together, these discourses discursively construct and normalise particular etiquette between pupils and teachers. Where a teacher or a pupil is constructed as behaving outside of this discourse, then he or she may be constructed as deviant.

The normalisation of beliefs and behaviours through discourse and the way in which things can be said and thought are of particular relevance. This highlights the difficulty that a person might have if they were to contest a particular discourse, not only because of the possible challenges to their thinking but also, perhaps, more significantly, because of the repercussions and responses of others to their critical comments or behaviours. Arguing against or behaving outside the dictates of a particular discourse may be both testing and risky. As Hook acknowledges, to do so is "to be mad, to be beyond comprehension and therefore reason" (Hook 2001, p. 2). As will be discussed later, for some boys, in certain circumstances, challenging particular masculine dominant discourses is acutely problematic.

Of particular interest for this study is the manner in which discourses define what can be said, thought and done. Discourses defining gender are a huge part of this. Lawler's (2008) comment about discourse and gender is particularly pertinent. She says:

> In the Foucauldian sense, gendered persons, and gender itself, are categories "made up" within discourses. Further, it is in the heterosexual encounter that gender gets "consecrated". . . . The notion of heterosexuality, we might say, "produces" . . . two distinct genders, which are kept apart conceptually.
>
> *(Lawler 2008, p. 117)*

Jupp and Norris contend that Foucault did not regard discourse "as a resource to explain the world but as an object of inquiry in its own right" (Jupp and Norris 1993, p. 39). This point is particularly significant because, as will be shown, understanding the discourses which people draw upon allows investigation into how "right and wrong" are constructed within different places, by different people, within varying cultures and in different institutions. So what is considered "wrong" in one place may not be so in another, and likewise, what is deemed "correct" within a culture, place or institution may be considered inappropriate in another.

Children coming to school will draw upon a variety of discourses in relation to socialising, attitudes towards learning, eating, play, anger management and various other behaviours predominantly learnt at home and within their own communities. If the discourses pupils draw upon are at odds with those of other pupils or staff in the school, then conflict might arise. But this will depend upon what Jupp and Norris (1993) refer to as the hierarchy of competing discourses and significantly how the credibility of one discourse over another is established and accepted.

The issue of competing discourses is important. Of particular significance is how one discourse is more powerful than another, resulting in conflict or the subjugation of one discourse over another. Thus, in questioning what actually counts as truth, Foucault says:

> Each society has its regime of truth, its "general politics" of truth: that is, the types of discourse which it accepts and makes function as true; the mechanisms and instances which enable one to distinguish true and false statements, the means by which each is sanctioned; the techniques and procedures accorded value in the acquisition of truth; the status of those who are charged with saying what counts as true.
>
> *(Foucault 1980, p. 131)*

Power

During this discussion about discourse, several references to power, knowledge and truth have been made. This is unsurprising because, as Foucault states, "truth[s] are produced within discourses which in themselves are neither true nor false" (Foucault 1980, p. 118). And further to this, Foucault also says, "power produces knowledge" [and] "power and knowledge directly imply one another" (Foucault 1977, p. 27). Carabine, discussing Foucault's work, concisely explains his perspective:

> knowledges are socially constructed and produced by effects of power and spoken of in terms of "truths". Foucault argues that power is constituted

> thorough discourses. Thus, power is important in the construction of knowledge and what counts as knowledge.
>
> *(Carabine 2001, p. 275)*

The implication that there are links among power, knowledge, truth and discourse is very significant because discourses are regularly drawn upon as a source of knowledge and presented and relied upon as true. As such, certain actions and behaviours of people are often explained as natural and normal, with people drawing upon discourses to present an argument of truth. Understanding why and how this occurs is important in understanding how problematic masculine behaviours in society and schools are encouraged, justified and validated.

To explore this further, it is necessary to understand what Foucault meant by "power". Kendall and Wickham say of Foucault's philosophical formations, "Power is a strategy concerned with relations between the sayable [and] . . . the visible" (Kendall and Wickham 1999, p. 55). While this explains that power defines what can be said and done under particular circumstances, it does not fully explain how power operates in all circumstances. Prado (2000) offers some clarification when he says that power:

> is the complex network of acts of domination, submission and resistance. Power constrains actions, not individuals. Power is a totality made up of individuals being dominated, coerced, or intimidated; of individuals submitting to domination, coercion, or intimidation; and of individuals resisting domination, coercion, or intimidation. Power is all about people acting in ways that blindly and impersonally condition the options and actions of others.
>
> *(Prado 2000, p. 37)*

Therefore, by drawing upon particular "discourses" and arguing that the statements in that "discourse" constitute something desirable and good, people in positions of power and domination promote those particular discourses which are beneficial to them. For example, in a classroom, it might be considered "good" to be quiet and listen to the teacher, particularly from the teacher's point of view. This correlates with Nietzsche (1913), who, discussing "good and evil and good and bad", argues that "good" is reasoned by those in positions of power and importance. They determine what is "good", based upon their views and the use such "good" might be to them. This argues that the "good", or the "statement" made within a discourse, is constructed by the person or institution with "power".

Power is central to the production of knowledge and truth. Of this, Smart acknowledges that "where power is exercised . . . knowledge is produced" (Smart 1983, p. 65). As such, discourses produced within an institution may be drawn upon and used as truth. As an example of this, commenting on the power afforded to the media and the influence that the media has on public opinion, Mills and Keddie warn that:

> The media is not a harmless commentator on public events. It works to construct the realities of which it writes.
>
> *(Mills and Keddie 2010, p. 440)*

This acknowledges that the media is afforded power, which enables its discourses to be considered as truth. However, the power and authority of government also enable their statements to be considered as true and thus can also be subsumed as discourses. The power afforded to school, government and media discourses and the belief in the truth of these discourses are particularly significant because determined within a discourse are suggestions that it offers a particular truth or particular truths.

There is much academic debate about natural and normal behaviour and child development. MacNaughton (2005), for example, discusses and challenges theories of "normal" child development and concepts of "normal" parenting, while authors such as Thorne (1993) discuss the social pressures upon boys and girls to behave and play in particular ways so as to conform to gender norms. It will be shown later in the narratives of boys and school staff how they drew upon discourses of truth to explain and justify actions and beliefs, using normative discourses to socially construct some boys as inadequate, or deviant, failing or disruptive and their parents as feckless and/or poorly skilled.

Social constructionism

Having considered Foucault's (1980) argument that knowledge is produced within sites of power and how such knowledge may be normalised as reality and become discourse, it is now possible to explore how discourse and social constructionism are interwoven.

Referring to reality, Berger and Luckmann argue that "reality is socially constructed" (Berger and Luckmann 1966, p. 13). By this, they mean that which is taken for granted as true and real is an interpretation, a ranking and evaluation, defined and agreed upon by people, drawing on discourse. Gergen refers to this process as "the result of an active, cooperative enterprise of persons in relationship" (Gergen 2003, p. 15). He adds that how people come to "describe, explain or otherwise account for the world" defines social constructionism. This explains that what we define as right or wrong, and how we describe good and bad, and indeed how boys define each other and how men and women are characterised, is done through social agreements and by drawing upon particular discourses. These discourses may have been formed around arbitrary standards and historical cultural norms or designed to serve the purpose of an institution or person(s) of power. Such discourses and social constructions have one thing in common: they are "things that exist only because we believe them to exist" (Searle 1995, p. 1).

Of particular importance are the views of Johnson (1997) and Connell (1995), who illustrate how gender is also an example of a social construct, utilising binary discourses of behaviour, attitudes and abilities.

Education policy discourse also contributes towards particular constructions of normality. An example of this is education policy determining the minimum educational achievements required for 16-year-old pupils (DfE 2011, 2014c). This has the effect of constructing normalised pupils who achieve the minimum standards and, in doing so, also of constructing those not achieving as failures. As discussed earlier, the effects upon those who fail at school may have a profound impact upon their later choices in life and, for some boys, the educational and career choices they make. This is because pupils who differ from socially constructed norms, such as school achievement, may potentially be socially constructed as abnormal or deviant, even when such standards are considered to have been reached arbitrarily, as Ball (2006) argues.

The connection of power and social construction is most important because, as Vance (1995) explains, social construction is the manner in which people, or an institution, define, label and categorise someone or something. As was discussed earlier, power affords knowledge and truth; therefore, the constructions made within positions of power are harder to contest.

The concept of dominant masculinity as normal is a significant issue for some boys and schools: from the boys' perspective, as being obliged to accommodate and mimic such behaviour, and from the perspective of the school and staff, as having to handle resulting behaviours constructed as disruptive. Understanding how discourses and social constructions establish normality is fundamental to the structure of this book. As Burr (1995) argues, if we take a:

> critical stance towards our taken-for-granted ways of understanding the world. . . . It invites us . . . to challenge the view that conventional knowledge is based upon objective, unbiased observation of the world.
>
> *(Burr 1995, p. 3)*

"We are able to unmask the regimes of truth that govern us precisely because it is we who hold them in place and reproduce them" (MacNaughton 2005, p. 39).

Gergen and Gergen (2003) argue that our commonly held assumptions about good and bad serve as anchors for our daily activities. Such truths and anomalies are contained in what Garfinkel (2003) refers to as common discourses. He explains that where these discourses are drawn upon, users assume that they are universally accepted and understood. Garfinkel suggests that there is an:

> anticipation that people *will* understand, the occasionality of expressions, the specific vagueness of references, the retrospective- prospective sense of a present occurrence, waiting for something later in order to see what was meant before, are sanctioned properties of common discourse.
>
> *(Garfinkel 2003, p. 12)*

Foucault argued that logic, views and opinions are shaped by social and cultural influences, which are in turn affected by power and knowledge (Foucault 1970, 1972, 1980).

In relation to the views and comments of boys and school staff, this approach is particularly valuable in understanding how dominant masculine behaviours are normalised and constructed as truths. As Pattman and Kehily (2004) argue

> There are many different social constructionist perspectives on gender. However they all share the idea that becoming male or female is a social process that is learned through culture: in the family, in school and in social interactions more generally.
>
> *(Pattman and Kehily 2004, p. 132)*

4

CONSTRUCTIONS OF HEGEMONIC MASCULINITY

Having discussed how the male species of the human race is responsible for a great deal of damaging and destructive behaviours and how ideas about masculinity are embedded in "discourse", I now wish to explore academic literature to determine the normality or otherwise of this matter. This literature will be used later in the analysis of interviews with school staff and male pupils.

To begin with, consideration is given to the academic literature on masculinities, peer interactions and the means by which various authors discuss and construct boys' behaviour. Connected with this is a review of literature discussing the origins of the role model discourse and how it is variously referred to as a universal remedy to those boys' behaviours, which are constructed as problematic. This is followed by a review of literature examining how parenting and parenting skills are attributed to influencing boys' behaviour and attitudes towards school and their adoption of certain masculine behaviours.

The prehistoric tradition

In our society, there are preferred versions of masculinity that are considered to be normal and natural and which are used to construct the characteristics and attributes of men and women as distinctly different and, in particular, to maintain the position of men as superior. Disputing the normality of such gendered behaviours, Connell maintains that these versions are produced through discourses, which define what "true" masculinity is and is not and how men should and should not behave. While such essentialist definitions of masculine behaviours continue to be considered by some as natural and

DOI: 10.4324/9781003732785-5

normal, academics such as Butler (1993), McGuffey (1999), Reay (2002), Paechter (2007), Fine (2010) and Francis (2012) argue that masculinity is a performance, learnt, rehearsed and enforced through culture, peer groups and families. Thus, Connell explains, "gender must be understood as a social structure. It is not an expression of biology" (Connell 2009, p. 9).

The fragility of essentialist hegemonic discourses which support the superiority of males over females and normalise particular male behaviours is well documented by authors such as Diamond and Quinby (1988), Thorne (1993), Kehily and Nayak (1997), Renold (1997), Francis and Skelton (2001) and Connell (2009). They discuss how boys, families, teachers and the media promote discourses that normalise dominant masculinities and marginalise and denigrate females and those boys who do not conform. Discussing gender binaries and constructions of what Mills (2001) refers to as the "ideal man", authors such as Delgardo and Stefancic (1995), Johnson (1997), Haywood (2003) and Connell (1995) list the attributes and behaviours that the "ideal man" displays. These include strength, control, competitiveness, sexual competence and risk-taking. Women are constructed in opposition to these characteristics.

Volman and Dam (1998) suggest that the normalisation of hegemonic masculine behaviours and the construction of gender binary asymmetries are historical products. Diamond and Quinby (1988) argue that such patriarchal arguments hide cultural constructions of power by expressing them as natural. Discussing this further, Johnson suggests that, "Given thousands of years of patriarchal history, it's easy to slide into the belief that things have always been this way" (Johnson 1997, p. 224), and therefore will remain so. This historical normalisation and the accompanying male violence are referred to by Mills as a "prehistoric tradition" (Mills 2001).

The existence of such a "prehistoric tradition" cannot be denied. Although some authors might attempt to trivialise the idea of this, Jablonka (2019) does not. While not accepting the legitimacy of male dominance and patriarchy, he nevertheless describes and explains how it has happened, discussing the origins of our patriarchal societies and, thus, how and why men have maintained their position of dominance and power for so long. The apparent societal acceptance of this and the resulting longevity are often used as a means of normalising the existence of male dominance, male differences and their supposed superiority over women. However, Jablonka does not do this; instead, he explains that male dominance throughout history has been sustained through men's use of strength, violence and misogyny. While this may be true, it has also been maintained through men's use of their accepted power to manipulate male and female work and recreation.

An example of this is illustrated by the 1841 "Mines and Collieries Act", banning women from working underground in coal mines. At the time, it was reasoned that the male physique and temperament were better suited to the work than those of women. Lord Londonderry is also reported as saying that the employment of women in coal mines was inconsistent with their "family duties". Paxman argues that the banning of women working underground was done to preserve the work for men and to maintain male dominance in society, not because women were truly unsuitable or unable to do the work (Paxman 2021).

A further example is shown in sport. Women's football was both popular and enthusiastically attended before, during and after the First World War. But then, in 1921, the Football Association demanded that clubs stop women from using their grounds, effectively preventing women from playing. This ban was based upon the idea that a "woman's physical frame" was unsuitable for the sport (BBC.co.uk 2014). However, with the current resurgence and success of women's football, it is difficult to see how the reasoning for this ban had any honest logical merit.

What these two pieces of history show us is how male dominance has been purposefully and artificially maintained and preserved over the years and, in doing so, how this has then encouraged and maintained the "prehistoric tradition" discussed earlier.

As history illustrates, men have for centuries had the dominant narrative, and as such, women in history have been largely erased or ignored, thus insuring that the dominant masculine story prevails. Ignoring the historical contribution of women secures and preserves the male-dominant position (English 2021). Where in history women have been successful or have held positions of power, they are often then either demonised for their success or presented as being unique in having masculine characteristics.

One example of such a characterisation is Margaret Thatcher. She served as Prime Minister from 1979 to 1990, and because of her apparent steadfastness and strength of character, she was known in the media as the "iron lady" (Williams 2020). The media implication was that her strength of leadership of the Conservative Party and as Prime Minister of the United Kingdom could not have been achieved without her possession and display of masculine characteristics, rather than any feminine attributes. What this characterisation effectively does is marginalise and then destroy any feminine input but reinforce the importance and significance of dominant masculinity and therefore further reinforce the "prehistoric tradition".

The masculine dominant discourse has been further nurtured in another manner. Similar to Connell, Timimi argues that Western culture is driven by masculine macho ideals, which she claims are driven by discourse, "including the powerful influence of the media" (Timimi 2005, p. 87). Considering this contention, it can therefore be argued that the media, in particular TV and film, propagate the myth of male strength and superiority and in doing so contribute towards perpetuating patriarchy and the "prehistoric tradition".

If we consider data regarding motion pictures, it confirms that overall, 77% of films feature more male than female characters in speaking roles (Lauzen 2023). Such male dominance of film has the potential to further reinforce ideas of male dominance and superiority. Further to this, it has also been shown that women are often stereotyped and sexualised when featured in films. They also rarely hold positions of power or importance on screen (Smith et al. 2014). In an analysis of films awarded an Oscar, Johnson shows that only four out of 40 films told a story through the life of a woman (Johnson 1997, p. 11). This apparent devaluing of females on film has the potential to enhance hegemonic perceptions. This should be of concern because, as Smith et al. (2014) also argue, research demonstrates that media images can shape both boys' and girls' perceptions of themselves.

When we consider the information above, it can be seen that not only does the media have the potential to influence the views and characteristics of children, but it can also be seen how the historical patriarchal tradition has the potential to be normalised, validated and thus reinforced by particular representations of men and women on film and TV.

Further to this, various popular UK media, newspapers and policy discourses frequently normalise aspects of boys' behaviour and claim that boys are naturally different from girls. Newspaper articles such as "Ministers tell nurseries to allow boys toy guns" (Woolcock 2007) and government documents such as "Confident, capable and creative: supporting boys' achievements" (DCSF 2007a) have the potential to contribute towards constructing certain boys' behaviour as natural and therefore risk reinforcing gendered binaries.

In relation to media involvement, a 2021 article in GQ magazine somewhat dismissively admitted that there was an association with what they referred to as "alpha male-ness" and the eating of hot curry. They also claimed that studies had found that hot curry eating might be linked to male behaviours such as risk-taking, attention-seeking and thrill-seeking behaviours that young men have been found to be predisposed to (Staples 2021). It is therefore unsurprising that some men perceive that their ability to eat a chilli-hot curry is a sign of masculine toughness and thus a sign of manliness. Curry eating might not appear to be a particularly important or problematic issue, and we can dismiss this just as we tend to dismiss many of the obtuse behaviours that we attribute to men. In fact, using a historical norm, many of those I interviewed did just that, accepting that much male behaviour was problematic but at the same time dismissing it as normal. While the article in GQ magazine discussed men and curry eating, it then appeared to be dismissive of the whole idea of "alpha male-ness", and I presume any associated problematic behaviours associated with it. While this magazine's influence might be construed as trivial, it does further illustrate views, opinions and the range of masculine discourse which exists within society.

Discussing male violence, Mills suggests that there is an assumption that there is a "unitary masculinity which serves as a blueprint for normal masculinities" (Mills 2001, p. 53) and that this masculinity is the preserve of boys and men. This is supported by authors such as Halberstam (1998) and Paechter (2006a, 2006b, 2007), adding that particular behaviours, such as aggression, strength and competitiveness, continue to be constructed as uniquely masculine. However, in contrast, Francis (2010, 2012) draws attention to "gender heteroglossia", the coexistence of male and female behaviours in men and women, and in doing so further challenges the construction of hegemonic masculinities as being uniquely male, natural or normal.

However, despite evidence to the contrary, dominant masculine discourses and the normalising of the "prehistoric tradition" remain powerful within particular communities, among some boys, and in the media and government policy. How boys and educational practitioners consider such discourses will be explored in the later interview analysis.

Striving to be the "ideal man"

What we have is an idea that, structured within the dominant masculine discourses and the historical norms discussed earlier, is the assumption that there exists a perfect man, with skills and attributes which all men should admire and aim to achieve.

Much academic research argues that masculinity is not essentialist or normal but is a performance, a social construction, which is learnt, rehearsed and enforced through culture, peer groups and family (Butler 1990, 1993; Tilsen et al. 2007; Francis 2010, 2012). Such academic work argues that our understanding of gender and the accepted behaviour of men should be understood as a social construction and not an expression of biology (Connell 2009). Francis argues that hegemonic masculinity is constructed in opposition to femininity (Francis 2000); thus, anything considered to be feminine is deemed by those men/boys adopting this position as unacceptable.

There is some longevity in this social construction of maleness. This is shown by the nineteenth-century nursery rhyme, discussed earlier, which illustrates, as Francis argues, how boys were then constructed in opposition to girls, with boys being disagreeable and girls being pleasant.

What are little boys made of?
Snips, snails and puppy dogs' tails.

What are little girls made of?
Sugar and spice and all things nice.

Men do not, it seems, see themselves like this. Masculine ideals construct the qualities of men as having control, strength, efficiency, competitiveness, toughness and coolness under pressure (Johnson 1997). One academic refers to this set of attributes as "The ideal man", arguing that Western society promotes and encourages boys and men to adopt particular male characteristics and behaviours which they consider "perfect" or "ideal" (Mills 2001, p. 23). It is suggested that the "ideal man" not only possesses a range of attributes as discussed earlier but also includes a willingness to engage in risk-taking activities (Brittan 1989; Kehily and Nayak 1997; Epstein et al. 2001; Skelton 2001; Ludden 2020). As Bourdieu says, "Manliness . . . (is) constructed in front of and for other men and against femininity" (Bourdieu 2001, p. 53). Consequentially, boys who cannot or do not conform to the attributes discussed earlier are constructed as weak and inferior (Renold 2002; Smith et al. 2004).

Similar to others, this "historical" normalisation and the accompanying male violence are referred to as a "prehistoric tradition" (Mills 2001), a position verified but not legitimised by Jablonka (2019). As discussed earlier, Jablonka explains that thousands of years of patriarchy were maintained through male strength, dominance, violence and aggression, attributes which some men deem as normal and desirable. As a consequence, the power and the normality attributed to such behaviours encourage the need for some men and boys to be obliged to continue to prove their masculinity in their quest to be an "ideal man". The term "ideal man" will be referred to throughout this book.

Men and nature nurture

The weight of evidence shows that males are far more likely than females to engage in disruptive, damaging and illegal problematic behaviours. As the statistics are so huge, historically long-lasting and overwhelming, it is difficult not to assume that these problematic behaviours are somehow normal for men. And despite academic arguments to the contrary, there are those who continue to normalise differences in the behaviours of men and women. An example of this comes from the Australian government, which suggests that boys need to be taught differently from girls (Martino and Pallotta-Chiarolli 2007). Such a proposal reinforces the normality of particular forms of masculinity. It does so without considering the social pressures upon boys, which might be contributing towards their apparent unique educational needs.

Other academics support the view that men are naturally different from women in their thinking and behaviours. For example, some neuropsychologists (Gurian 2001; Baron-Cohen 2003; Gurian and Stevens 2005; Knickmeyer et al. 2005; Sax 2005) argue that boys' thinking, development and behaviours are biologically and naturally unlike those of girls. In particular, they contend that men's brains are "wired" differently compared to women's, and thus, they possess particular abilities and behaviours, some of which, they say, explain and account for the problems discussed. More recently, Reeves, discussing the difficulties boys face in education and their apparent academic failure, has argued that sex differences shape bodies and psychology. Reeves adds that men are typically more aggressive and take more risks than girls (Reeves 2022). Such normalising assumptions are widely challenged by other academic studies (Titus 2004; Lorber 2005; Fine 2010).

Significantly, what is not acknowledged by Baron-Cohen and others is the environmental influences that contribute towards boys' and men's behaviours and attitudes, specifically the pressures upon boys/men to behave in these particular ways.

Further to this and by comparison, work by Sharon Moalem presents a different and more challenging argument, stating that genetically, men are different from women, being genetically weaker at both the beginning and the end of life. Women, he states, generally appear to live longer than men regardless of education or economics (Moalem 2020). However, while discussing particular differences, Moalem does not relate genetic differences to explain aggressive male problematic behaviours.

Our society associates a range of attributes to describe males and females differently; however, for the most part, these attributes lack both a biological or genetic explanation (Harari 2014) and therefore do not explain the aggression and violence that is associated with men.

Some academics argue that long-standing persuasive statistics about problematic male behaviour induce a social belief that such aggressive, dominant and violent behaviours and attitudes are normal and natural in men, and indeed, many men and some women believe this to be true. But how can this be so? In suggesting and accepting this, we are ignoring the fact that it is not all men that murder, steal and have accidents, and neither are all boys at school problematic and disruptive in class; it is a proportion. The question about male behaviour and whether all men are aggressive, violent and deviant needs careful scrutiny, particularly if, when considering this information, we are accepting and normalising this behaviour and thus implying that it is not only normal but also desirable for men to behave so.

It appears that our society apathetically recognises the problematic behaviours of men and, to a degree, acknowledges the consequential emotional, physical and financial harm that is inflicted on individuals and society. However, there does not appear to be a significant social or media debate about the normality or otherwise of these behaviours. To me, it is nevertheless clear that this is a major issue which requires urgent attention.

It was suggested at the beginning of this book that a visiting alien, observing the damaging male behaviours discussed earlier, might conclude that men, compared to women, are a deviant and destructive species who are overwhelmingly responsible for a range of societal problems. Indeed, when considering the information above, there is a temptation to conclude, as the nineteenth-century nursery rhyme suggests, that boys really are made from unpleasant stuff.

I will show that there is an alternative explanation. What I shall be exploring in the following pages is the notion that within the culture of the Western world, there is an imbedded belief that there is a single and superior form of masculinity to which all boys should aspire and that society widely, and somewhat unknowingly, seeks to reinforce this particular form of masculinity. I will show that this "ideology" both encourages and accepts aggression, violence, dominance and strength as normal and, moreover, desirable and that by endorsing these attributes, we are purposefully reinforcing the idea that for a boy or man to behave otherwise is weak and unacceptable. I shall later further discuss the powerful influences upon men to adopt aggression and risk-taking activities in order to "prove" that they are masculine.

Disruptive and incompatible boys' behaviours in schools

A combination of boys' poor behaviour in school, lack of achievement and educational failure is highly significant in contributing to the perpetuation of problematic masculine behaviours throughout society. We also know that boys' educational failure is often linked to crime and prison (Evans and Wallace 2007; Colman et al. 2009).

Although academics dismiss the normalisation of hegemonic masculinity, Epstein et al. (1998), Gilbert and Gilbert (1998) and Arnot et al. (1999) acknowledge that some boys' construction of themselves within this dominant discourse influences their attitude to gender and their masculinity, as well as attitudes towards education and authority. Discussing how this affects their behaviour in school, Francis says a "social constructionist argument [is] that pupils' constructions of gender produce different behaviours which impact on achievement" (Francis 2009, p. 646). Connell (2009), Mills (2001) and Pattman et al. (1998) suggest that boys' gendered acts are often demonstrated through what are determined as disruption, aggression and violence, and it is these performances which schools construct as incompatible and are often cited as contributory factors leading towards boys' exclusion from schools (Arnold et al. 2009; DCSF 2009; Pirrie et al. 2009; Millham et al. 1975).

Government policy and advisory reports frequently give guidance to schools on matters of pupil behaviour, particularly that of boys. A 2005 DfES report placed emphasis upon schools developing "Codes of conduct" (Steer 2005), while current DfE advice to schools stresses the maintenance of "good" pupil behaviour (DfE 2014a). The implementation of "codes of conduct" and "good" behaviour relies upon the skill, the power and the authority of staff. Where boys draw on hegemonic masculine discourses, or what

Halberstam (1998) and Reay (2002) refer to as working-class masculinities, it would appear that confrontation in school is inevitable, not least because, as Foucault argues, "Where there is power, there will be resistance" (Foucault 1976, p. 95). Boys' resistance to the disciplinary regime of schools is well documented by authors such as Archer et al. (2005) and Timimi (2005).

Lareau (2003) suggests that one of the major reasons for confrontation in schools is that they are organised around middle-class ideals and values, which include negotiation and non-violence. These attributes are at odds with some working-class families. Peal (2014), discussing poor behaviour in schools, draws on data from the *Elton Report* (1989), which suggests that most teachers rely on negotiation and non-punitive methods when dealing with discipline problems. Such middle-class approaches may be at odds with some boys' constructions of discipline, particularly those who draw on discourses of hegemonic masculinities to make sense of themselves and construct how they should respond towards authority, confrontation and peers. Boys' behaviour in schools is pertinent in understanding the relationship between boys and men and constructions of hegemonic masculinity throughout society.

Masculinities, peer interactions and teachers

Authors including McLean (1995), Mills (2001) and Chambers et al. (2004) argue that interactions between boys can contribute towards problematic displays of physical and verbal behaviours. It is argued that some boys engage in policing, peer pressure and bullying to show how "masculine" they are and encourage other boys to comply with dominant masculinity within environments such as schools.

Green (2007) notes that there are two types of bullying in schools, physical and verbal. Supporting this observation, Murlidhar and Shastri, while acknowledging that both boys and girls engage in aggression in schools, note that boys were more likely to display physical aggression, while girls were more likely to use verbal aggression (Murlidhar and Shastri 2016). Traore's report on pupils in French schools echoes this (Traore 2022), while a UNICEF report discussing peer violence also states that boys are more likely to be subjected to peer violence than girls (UNICEF 2017). This issue is clearly an international problem.

Discussing this matter further, McLean (1995) explains that physical strength is considered by some boys as one of the major signifiers of manhood. Therefore, to be constructed as a man by peers and oneself, some boys perceive the need to display and prove that they are physically strong. This often results in physical bullying. Supporting previous statements, Green (2007) says that 89% of physical bullying in schools is perpetrated by boys upon other boys. However, where boys use verbal abuse, Pascoe (2007) and

Chambers et al. (2004) explain that it then includes misogynistic and homosexual insults. This is done to further encourage male peers to conform to particular versions of hegemonic masculinity and, in particular, to denigrate those who do not.

Authors such as Kane (2011), Sherriff (2007), Smith (2007), Holland et al. (1993) and Thorne (1993) highlight the pressure of such bullying upon boys to adopt and engage in hegemonic behaviours. Discussing this, Connell (2009) argues that not only is there pressure upon them to conform, but also additional pressure is placed upon men and boys who cannot or will not conform. Explaining the physical and verbal violence, which often accompanies bullying and masculine performances, Mills says:

> violence by males against males, which is often interpreted as boys being boys or as bullying, is indeed gender based. Such violence is often a form of boundary policing, usually with a homophobic edge, which serves to both normalise particular constructions of masculinity while also determining where a boy is positioned within a hierarchical arrangement of masculinities.
>
> *(Mills 2001, p. 4)*

While it is claimed that peer interactions have the potential to adversely affect the choices and behaviours boys engage in, authors such as Barnes (2012), Haywood and Mac-an-Ghaill (2003), Francis and Skelton (2001) and others suggest that some teachers' actions also have the potential to exacerbate and encourage what Connell (2005) refers to as hegemonic masculinity. They do this through discipline methods, competition and encouragement of particular peer group interaction. Barnes' (2012) study indicates how male teachers use hegemonic masculine behaviours and "laddishness" to keep boys in order or to get them on their side. In an earlier study, Francis and Skelton (2001) discussed how male teachers use homophobia and sexism to enhance their position and as a means of discipline. This suggests that influences upon boys to adhere to forms of dominant masculinity come not just from other boys but from some teachers as well. As Haywood and Mac-an-Ghaill argue, teaching styles and discipline methods influence boys' formations of identity. They add:

> disciplinary regimes of schools create specific kinds of men . . . tough teachers make tough boys . . . schools that adopt violent teaching practices generate schoolboy masculinities based upon competitive machismo.
>
> *(Haywood and Mac-an-Ghaill 2003, p. 64)*

So, while middle-class discipline values (discussed earlier) may be at odds with working-class boys, it is also argued that teachers who display what might be determined as hegemonic masculinity may exacerbate or reinforce dominant masculine discourses in some boys, therefore possibly influencing not only some boys' attitudes to school and learning but also their views on masculinity and patriarchy.

Parenting

Although school is an arena where, it is argued, boys learn and practise their masculinity, there are other areas of influence upon them. There is a broad assumption that parenting, and significantly the place of a father, is particularly important in a boy's life (Mulligan et al. 1963; Smith 2004; Scott et al. 2010; Assarsson and Aarsand 2011). Firstly, it is believed that children learn from the instructions that parents impose upon them. It is also believed that children witness the behaviours and values of their parents, and through these observations, they learn what they assume are appropriate values and correct ways to interact with others. There is also the strong belief that boys observe, imitate and adopt behaviours and values from their fathers. Research into what are considered "parenting skills" also claims that some parents are better skilled than others. Significantly, working-class parenting is often demonised, thus constructing middle-class parenting as somehow better (Ball 2008; Tyler 2008; Jones 2011). Politicians and the media play a particular role in these evaluations. For instance, a newspaper article by Frank Field[1] (2010) is an example of this discourse. The title of the article, "The biggest crisis facing Britain? Too many parents don't have a clue how to raise children", concisely reflects the constructions above.

The Western belief about childhood and parenting suggests that children are vulnerable and dependent upon their parents, and therefore, without parental guidance, boys cannot develop adequately. This in turn therefore reinforces the conviction that children are not born with an innate sense of self and/or an understanding of how to be an adult. If this is so, this further strengthens the argument that boys *learn how to be a man*, and therefore, particular male behaviours are not innate or inevitable.

However, there is also a fear among some parents of having a son who is not quite man enough and, in particular, a fear that he might not be able to defend himself (Doherty 2017). The question then arises as to how we ascertain which behaviours, values and attributes are correct and essential for boys to possess and therefore which should be rejected.

A relationship is often drawn between the behaviour of boys and what are constructed as parenting skills. UK government reports such as Steer (2005) and DCSF (2008) emphasise the involvement and responsibility of parents in their children's behaviour in school, but reports also seek to demonise and blame the parents of children whose behaviour falls below that deemed adequate (Mayer 2001; Scott et al. 2010). In exploring the responsibilities of parents, it is necessary to understand what is meant by the terms "child" and children's "needs".

While, in the United Kingdom, it is determined that a child is anyone below the age of 18 years (NSPCC 2012), academics such as Cannella (1997) argue that the term *child* is a social construction. The Western social construction of childhood and parenting constructs children as vulnerable and dependent upon their parents. James and James (2004) argue that this view is founded upon a social and political construction of, and normalisation of, children's "needs". How boys consider the construction of themselves as children has a significant impact on much of their behaviour.

Attending school is one of these "needs", with government policy defining where, when and how the child goes to school. In relation to these "needs", MacNaughton (2005), referring to Foucault, argues that ways of seeing, thinking and feeling about childhood have become developmental truths, which have become authoritative discourses. Woodhead (1997) adds that these discourses are so generally accepted that they are rarely questioned, adding that the "needs" of children, and what parents are responsible for, depend upon the social and cultural position of those making assumptions and judgements. Assarsson and Aarsand (2011) add that constructions of good parenting do not take into account the effects of culture. Katz et al. (2007) also argue that particular parents may be judged as good parents in their community but judged as inadequate against middle-class norms. Mayer (1997) explains that because (economically) poor parents are at the bottom of the social hierarchy, their "norms, values and behaviours" are constructed as dysfunctional in the "dominant culture". This suggests that working-class "parenting" may therefore appear abnormal to middle-class parents and to some educational practitioners, particularly as middle-class values dominate schools (Lareau 2003).

Much academic work argues that the skills and abilities of parents directly affect the welfare and behaviour of children. Discussing this, Uprichard (2008) argues that a child is an "adult in the making", and it is the skills of the parents that will "shape" the child into a good or bad adult. Others support this construction of parenting. Lopez et al. (2008) draw a relationship between boys' behaviour and what they construct as "poor parenting". Similarly, a DES report by Scott et al. (2010) refers to what they determine as "negative parenting" influencing children's behaviour at school. These constructions of parenting draw a relationship between what is constructed as inconsistent discipline and harsh and aggressive parenting, which result in behaviours incompatible with school. Parental violence is also widely considered to affect children's behaviour at school. Herrenkohl et al.'s (2000) research argues that children are socialised by their parents, and where children are raised in what they construct as violent homes, then they are more likely to be violent themselves, with the resulting confrontation at school. Boys are particularly vulnerable to this.

Liabo and Richardson (2007) and Morrell and Murray (2003) maintain that boys are particularly susceptible to what is constructed as "poor parenting". Gavita et al. (2011) argue that parents are not trained in the skills necessary to raise children and that bad parenting includes not only hitting but also significantly excessive criticism and inadequate guidance. Lykken (2003) and Hess (1995) agree that where parents do not give their children what they construct as adequate and consistent guidance, then they are more prone to seek and rely upon their peers for support and thus be influenced by their values and beliefs. As some boys' peer relationships often revolve around performances of dominant aggressive masculinity, resulting peer influences have the potential to exacerbate behaviours associated with hegemonic masculinities, which in turn may lead to behaviours constructed as disruptive in school. This argument is particularly significant if, as Crosnoe et al. (2008) argue, peer pressure does not weaken with age. Recent UK exclusion statistics indicate that older boys are at greater risk of exclusion than younger pupils and girls (Cotzias 2014).

Discussing boys' behaviour further, Titus (2004) and Westwood (1996) argue that there is a moral panic about fatherless boys and what is constructed as feckless parents who are failing to raise their children well. Media discourses, such as Doughty (2013), and government discourses, such as Gove (2011), argue that parents, particularly fathers, should act as role models and advocate that male teachers could act in a compensatory role to boys. However, Clarke and Kitzinger contend that a father's importance and contribution to a family is an assumption which is "simply taken-for-granted" (Clarke and Kitzinger 2005). Donovan (2000) adds that the absent fatherhood debate is based upon patriarchal discourses, which construct fathers as economic providers and disciplinarians to children. Further to this, these authors' arguments suggest that media and government discourses seek to undermine the skills of single mothers and, in doing so, reaffirm a patriarchal dominant masculine discourse, a discourse which many normalise because of its apparent historical roots.

However, Cohen (2002) suggests that there has been a deliberate construction of an atmosphere of distrust, which has resulted in the demonising of unemployed parents as "welfare cheats" and "dole scroungers". Authors such as Jones (2011), Tyler (2008), Titus (2004) and Westwood (1996) explain how single mothers, the poor working class, absent fathers and the unemployed are constructed by some academics, politicians, political policy-makers and the media as inadequate and irresponsible in their relationships with and parenting of their children.

According to Assarsson and Aarsand, gender, generation and social class are problematic. What remains is a complicated and somewhat vague definition of the "needs" of children and of parenting skills, generated through discourse. Literature confirms Foucault's argument that power forms discourse and therefore determines what is to be constructed as good and desirable. In particular, it enables those with the most power to legitimise and normalise (Foucault 1980, 1982). This is reflected in media and policy discourses that demonise and blame the parents of children whose behaviour is constructed as problematic.

What has been suggested is that boys are particularly vulnerable to what has been determined as poor parenting and, where parenting is lacking, are more susceptible to the support and guidance of their peers (Hess 1995; Lykken 2003). As such, they are more exposed to and influenced by the good or bad values and beliefs their peers display and promote. As some boys' peer relationships often revolve around performances of dominant aggressive masculinity, resulting peer influences have the potential to exacerbate behaviours associated with hegemonic masculinities, which in turn may lead to behaviours constructed as disruptive in school. This argument is particularly significant if, as Crosnoe et al. (2008) argue, peer pressure does not weaken with age.

Much of my research for this book was concentrated on interviews with school staff and boy pupils. It showed that school was, and is, a powerful place where ideas about life and behaviour are learnt, adopted and reinforced (Banner 2015). One academic argument is that, before boys leave nursery school, stereotyped notions of masculinity have already been absorbed (Askew and Ross 1988). Although, undoubtedly, boys learn about masculinity from their families, I argue that school is also a particularly powerful and dominant environment. After all, school makes up a large proportion of a child's life and therefore unquestionably has a sizeable influence upon children. Let us consider, firstly, how and where boys learn about what it means to be a man and, consequentially, how they determine how they should or should not behave.

Peer pressure and bullying in schools

Human beings are social animals, and therefore, to be excluded from a social group is a difficult and painful experience. As Hay et al. (2004) argue, solitude is normally avoided by children at school. Unsurprisingly, for many boys at school, it is immensely important for them to be part of a social group; to maintain this, it is necessary for boys to comply with the rules and values of that group and the pressures that their peers inflict upon them. These pressures vary somewhat, but all include aspects of hegemonic masculinity. There is a list of attributes that boys in school aim to achieve and equally a list that they aim to avoid. As has been discussed, of overwhelming importance for a boy is to be seen by others as male, not female, and this is done by conforming to peer values and undertaking performances of what are valued as male behaviours. This includes regularly demonstrating that you are a heterosexual, not a homosexual. This notion is reinforced by acting and appearing tough, strong, aggressive and able to defend yourself. The "ideal man" also displays aspects of control, competitiveness and sexual competence. Importantly, in schools, challenges to a boy's manhood have to be defended. As a result, demonstrations of masculinity and challenges to it are a regular source of confrontation in schools. Examining the reasons for boys' exclusion from school provides further understanding of this particular issue.

As has been mentioned, boys are far more likely to be excluded from school than are girls, and there are a number of behaviours that result in exclusion from school. The most common problem is aggressive behaviour towards other students and teachers and a rejection of learning, leading to classroom disruption. As aggression is thought by some to be a necessary male attribute, dissecting these contentions will give further understanding.

Let us first consider bullying in schools. While bullying is an issue affecting both boys and girls, bullying of boys upon boys is a specifically different problem because, for schools, "boy" bullying more regularly involves the use of physical violence. In the run-up to the 2024 general election, the Labour Party proposed adding VAT to private school fees. This led to an outcry from some who argued the increased cost would force some parents to remove their children from private schools and place them in state schools. The Daily Mail published an article, apparently written by a 14-year-old, who feared leaving his private school because of the abundance of violence in state schools (Boy 2024).

In truth, there is bullying and violence among pupils in all types of schools, and bullying and peer pressure are not unique to UK schools. A recent report by Kumudha shows that peer pressure among adolescents in Indian schools had a profound negative influence on adolescent students. The report says that such peer pressure encouraged engagement in risky behaviours, antisocial behaviour and student disengagement from studies. Unsurprisingly, boys were more significantly impacted than girls (Kumudha 2025). This research indicates that the issue of hegemonic masculine bullying and subsequent peer pressure upon boys is not unique to the United Kingdom, Australia or the United States but is universal.

Academic studies consider that there are two types of bullying in schools, physical and verbal (Martino 1995; Smith et al. 2004). It has been shown that some boys use both types of bullying to demonstrate their "manhood" to others and to encourage other boys to comply with their particular notion of masculine behaviour. Physical strength, in particular, is considered by some boys as one of the main signifiers of the "ideal man", and therefore, in order to be accepted and seen as an "ideal man" by one's peers and oneself, some boys believe that they need to engage in aggression and violence towards other boys in order to demonstrate and prove that they are physically strong. Such behaviour often results in conflict and physical violence between boys.

Statistics show that 89% of physical bullying in schools is perpetrated by boys upon other boys. A boy engaging in bullying is often seeking to show others that he, as the perpetrator, is strong and therefore a man but, importantly, that the recipient is weak and is therefore less of a man. As McGuffey and Rich say, high-status boys use hegemonic masculinity to police others (McGuffey and Rich 1999).

Let us now consider both bullying and peer pressure in schools. The two things are both interlinked and sometimes the same. Peer pressure can be quite subtle, consisting of verbal, non-verbal and physical communications. "Communication" might appear an odd word to use here, but it is chosen carefully because, as I shall explain, physical and verbal bullying and peer pressure to conform are forms of communication.

But what is it that is being communicated? Firstly, while we understand that boys and girls are physically different, it is the concept that boys are somehow superior to girls that is being constantly communicated. Being the "ideal man" is the ambition. Academics suggest that masculinity, being a man, is defined by *what it is not*; in other words, as a boy you are heterosexual, and you are not a woman or a girl. Consequentially, insults from peers frequently include derogatory accusations of being feminine or homosexual. As a result of such peer insults, many boys avoid particular activities or do not admit to engaging in activities which are considered by some as feminine. In this respect, the bully/perpetrator is using these insults to communicate that he considers femaleness and homosexuality as inferior and particular types of masculinity as superior. Peers around him will support this communication, thus further cementing the hegemony of masculine behaviours and the inferiority of female traits.

Physical bullying is closely linked with verbal bullying, which is also a significant issue in schools (Smith et al. 2004). Name-calling, teasing, ridiculing and other forms of verbal abuse often include misogynistic and homophobic insults. As discussed, this is done to reinforce the notion that certain behaviours, attitudes and activities are the domain of men and, like aggressive masculinity (being the "ideal man"), are superior and desirable, while homosexuality and femininity are weak and unacceptable.

Physical bullying is often carried out as a challenge to the recipient, to demonstrate the perpetrator's manhood and to confirm the weakness of the victim. Such bullying also encourages onlooking male peers to conform to particular versions of hegemonic masculinity. Physical bullying denigrates those boys who do not or cannot conform or defend themselves. As mentioned, behaviours deemed as feminine, such as reading, art, music, pacifism and perhaps the wearing of particular clothing, are mocked and ridiculed, and those apparently displaying such behaviours are more likely to be subjected to intimidation and threats of aggression and violence. Academic studies highlight (Thorne 1993; Paechter 2007; Sherriff 2007; Smith 2007; Jones 2011) the pressure that such bullying places upon boys to adopt and engage in hegemonic behaviours. In particular (Connell 2009), not only is there pressure upon boys to conform, but also additional pressure is placed upon men and boys who cannot or will not conform, with resulting aggressive physical consequences. One academic says:

> violence by males against males, which is often interpreted as boys being boys or as bullying, is indeed gender based. Such violence is often a form of boundary policing, usually with a homophobic edge, which serves to both normalise particular constructions of masculinity while also determining where a boy is positioned within a hierarchical arrangement of masculinities.
>
> *(Mills 2001)*

What this means is that physical and verbal bullying is used to intimidate those boys who may appear "less masculine" than the peer group expects and certainly less so than the bully. The aggression reinforces the need for the boy to avoid being seen as feminine or homosexual by acting more macho and aggressive himself. The bully is at the same time showing his peers that he certainly is not feminine or homosexual. He is positioning himself above the weaker boy by demonstrating that he is strong and tough, while the behaviour of the other boy is seen as weak and unworthy. However, the bully in doing this has also placed himself in a position where he has to maintain his masculine status, so he may have to engage in further dominant masculine performances in order to do so.

What can be seen in the academic discussion above is how peer pressure among boys is a highly significant issue, reinforcing and securing ideas about male behaviours. It is clear that not all boys seriously misbehave at school or are meaningfully involved in risk-taking activities or behave in a dominant, aggressive or violent manner. However, as I shall illustrate, the pressure upon boys to commit to a particular single superior form of masculinity is immense, and schools, the home and the media all play a role in reinforcing the "ideal man" ideology.

Laddishness in schools

With literature about peer pressure in mind, it becomes possible to understand the reasons why some boys might reject education if it is perceived as feminine and as a challenge to their constructions of masculinity. It is also suggested that some boys may reject classes in which they feel unable to succeed and avoid tasks if they are likely to be ridiculed by friends for engaging in them. Archer et al. (2005), Jackson (2002, 2003), Covington (2000) and Archer and Yamashita (2003) argue that dismissing education, having a laugh, challenging teacher authority, being disruptive and so on are considered by some boys to be indicators of masculinity and therefore worthy attributes to possess. These behaviours may also be described as "laddishness", used to display aspects of dominant masculinity but also as a tactic to avoid engaging in education, risking failure or being perceived as feminine.

Jackson (2002, 2003), Covington (2000) and Francis (1999) explain that by drawing on particular discourses, some boys construct intelligence and learning as an attribute that ought to be innate for men. They consider that academic success should come naturally to men, and therefore, no effort is required or can be demonstrated. This is reinforced through discourse and peer pressure. They construct working hard academically as both feminine and a sign of masculine weakness and therefore refrain from showing their peers any signs of applying themselves academically. In addition, Arnot and Miles (2005) add that a competitive performance school system further encourages "laddish" culture because part of hegemonic masculinity is the inbuilt belief that, as a man, you should always win and come first. Subsequently, Covington (2000) and Jackson (2002) argue that because some boys view education as competitive, they will not try for fear of not coming first. Covington and Teel explain that "some students are motivated to avoid failure by not participating at all" (Covington and Teel 1996).

In summary, it is argued that laddishness is therefore a defence, a self-worth protection strategy, to protect against accusations of failure, lack of ability and being seen as feminine. As some boys' identity is based on their masculine status, "laddishness" allows them to cope with the fear of academic failure by utilising discourses of hegemonic masculine behaviours, which are accepted and admired in some masculine peer groups.

The role model discourse and boys' problem behaviours

We all may refer to role models at certain and particular times in our lives. A rudimentary understanding of a role model is that it is someone whom we admire, and we therefore observe and copy some of their characteristics and behaviours, thus modelling ourselves on them. As I will show, this is too simplistic an understanding.

The media and government ministers at various times simplistically suggest that providing schools with additional male staff would be a straightforward way of dealing with boys' educational performance and behaviours constructed as problematic. It assumes that male staff would act as role models for troublesome and under-achieving boys because there are no adequate male role models at home. These suggestions are based on discourses which construct single mothers as deficient and absent fathers as feckless while also arguing that the parenting skills of the working class are ineffective and detrimental (Westwood 1996; Cohen 2002).

The proposal for more male teachers returns to government and media discussions frequently. Indeed, in April 2025, the ex-England football manager, Gareth Southgate, made such a suggestion, arguing, in his BBC Richard Dimbleby Lecture, that boys needed positive role models and not the values promoted by online influencers. However, he also noted that boys tend to reject teachers as role models. Academic research agrees with this, indicating that promoting teachers as role models is based upon unsubstantiated theories (Cushman 2008).

The simplicity of this male role model proposal is explained by Clarke and Kitzinger, who argue that it is:

> so well embedded in our cultural common sense, that arguments about the necessity of male role models require little explanation or justification.
> *(Clarke and Kitzinger 2005, p. 148)*

To understand the implications of this, I will now discuss the origins of the role model discourse. It will be shown that the male role model proposal is ill conceived and based on ideas which fail to consider the intricacies of role modelling. It is first necessary to understand where and how these proposals emerged.

Merton first proposed his role model theory in 1957, with further work in the 1960s, 1970s and 1980s (Merton 1957, 1986; Cohen and Short 1961; Holton 2004). Merton's original work was a study of medical students where he argued that in seeking to define themselves within their chosen career, student physicians appraised themselves against established doctors of medicine. Merton theorised that people create "reference groups", consisting of a number of others, from whom characteristics are observed and chosen to emulate. In doing so, "they adopt a role model" (Merton 1957, p. 137).

There is a great deal of academic work that dismisses popular discourses around male role models as a solution to boys' difficulties at school (Mills et al. 2004; Bricheno and Thornton 2007; Cushman 2008). While many of the arguments put forward may appear credible, none address the issue from Merton's position. Merton argued that people choose role models, which suggests that role models cannot therefore be enforced.

The government and media's proposal to engage more male staff in schools to act as role models to disaffected boys is questioned by a number of academics. Mills et al. (2004) argue that current discourse for the recruitment and retention of male teachers is based on an assumption that men can offer something that women cannot. Jones (2003a) and Cushman (2008) suggest that the "something" men can offer is hegemonic masculinity. Mills et al.

(2008) refer to "an imaginary teacher" who "will act as a disciplinarian with unruly students, in particular boys" (Mills et al. 2008, p. 80).

It might be supposed that the government proposal for more male staff in schools would be based around the idea of offering boys the opportunity to observe men who *do not* construct themselves within a dominant masculine discourse and *do not* therefore present aggressive, hegemonic masculine behaviour. However, in a 2011 speech, Gove, the then Secretary of State for Education, said:

> We need more male teachers – especially in primary schools – to provide children who often lack male role models at home – with male authority figures who can display both strength and sensitivity.
>
> *(Gove 2011, p. 7)*

Mills et al. and Cushman argue that proposals such as Gove's have the potential to reinforce hegemonic masculinity while additionally marginalising female staff by constructing them as inadequate disciplinarians compared to men. Cushman concludes that the whole proposal is "grounded in unsubstantiated theories" (Cushman 2008, p. 133). In addition, I would suggest that such marginalising of female staff has the potential to enforce patriarchal discourses and thus reinforce further the discourse of "prehistoric tradition" as discussed earlier, citing the work of Mills (2001) and Jablonka (2019).

Other authors dismiss teachers as role models for different reasons. Bricheno and Thornton's (2007) research showed that pupils do not regard teachers as role models but instead look upon sportsmen, cinema actors, footballers and relatives for inspiration. They add that boys wish to emulate role models who have stereotypical characteristics, such as those who display strength, aggression and other hegemonic masculine behaviours. Statistics also undermine the role model proposal. Bricheno and Thornton (2007) indicate that only 2.4% of pupils interviewed referred to a teacher as a role model, while the work of Carrington et al. (2008) indicates that the gender of a teacher does not affect grades, attitude or achievement.

Gauntlett (2008), though not referring to Merton's work, contends that boys choose who they want as a role model based upon the discourse in which they position themselves. Hence, a role model needs to offer something desirable. Merton's work suggested that we create "reference groups" from which we select characteristics which we then copy and emulate. If this is so, we should be concerned about some of the characters that feature on film and TV.

There are occasionally complaints about the presentation on TV and cinema of tough and aggressive characters whose behaviour is presented as "cool" with the argument that such characters become role models (Line

2021). This should be of concern because, as Smith et al. (2014) argue, research demonstrates that media images can shape both boys' and girls' perceptions of themselves.

While we are aware that TV and film characters are fiction and therefore some may regard them as harmless entertainment, the features and characteristics they display do have the potential to act as powerful role models. As such, they have the potential to compound the myth that intelligence and learning are attributes that ought to be innate for men (Francis 1999; Jackson 2002, 2003).

Finally, if we consider Merton's role model theories, it can be seen how the dominance of men in cinema also has the potential to reinforce discourses which support and promote "prehistoric traditions" of patriarchal dominance and therefore perpetuate many of the problematic hegemonic masculine issues discussed at the beginning of this book.

Competition in schools

We live in a society where competition is widespread and deemed highly important. While some suggest that sport is to be enjoyed and taking part is what matters, competition nevertheless remains clearly overwhelmingly significant. Football matches, tennis tournaments and swimming races are, after all, either won or lost. But it is not just in sport where competition is rife.

In the wider society, competition exists in the high street, the stock exchange, the music industry, Hollywood and between political parties. It appears that competition is an essential, regular and normal part of human life. It is said that competition between supermarkets and other retail outlets encourages prices to be restrained and quality to be maintained. This is, apparently, a fundamental part of capitalism.

We can understand that winning or losing at Wimbledon contributes greatly towards the enjoyment of the tennis tournament. People support their football team, and their enjoyment is structured around watching them win their matches. But it is not all good news, as already mentioned; lost football matches contribute widely to male aggression and subsequent cases of domestic abuse. Being first holds very high societal value for men, and this is true for boys attending school, too.

Competition exists widely within the school system, with one school being measured as better than another, Ofsted evaluating the effectiveness of a school and an examination system which measures and grades the success or otherwise of students against fellow pupils. In this respect, schools are not simply establishments in which pupils are supposed to acquire skills for their adult life; it is argued that they are places where students are also graded for life (Ball 2003; Layard and Dunn 2009).

Being competitive and winning is a powerful characteristic of the "ideal man", and thus, losing is a particularly difficult issue for some boys and men to deal with. As was discussed earlier, losing is directly related to domestic abuse. Some academics argue that because competition is so prevalent in schools, this then encourages some boys to reject some subjects and classes where being first or best is not completely possible. It is also thought to encourage some boys' "laddish" culture. Research also shows that some boys may reject particular subjects and classes because of the fear of under-achievement. They may avoid subjects where they might not be first or achieve significantly or where they perceive that they might completely fail. Such avoidance is exacerbated if they are likely to be ridiculed by friends for engaging in a subject and then failing in it (Arnot and Miles 2005; Jackson 2002, 2003; Covington 2000; Ball 2003). Thus, peer pressure, together with a boy's own views about success and failure, plays a significant part in their participation in or avoidance of some subjects.

In addition, some consider that the "ideal man" is naturally gifted and intelligent. Learning and being taught are therefore deemed unnecessary because they consider that problem-solving is an attribute which ought to come naturally to boys and men. Failure in a subject therefore indicates weakness and a lack of manliness and may therefore result in some boys avoiding some subjects and/or demeaning a subject's significance in order to justify their lack of engagement therein. Demeaning subjects and non-participation are attempts to preserve their masculine mask. By not participating, it is then not possible to illustrate failure.

As suggested, for some boys, the act of dismissing education is in itself an act of masculinity. Added to which, being aggressive and disruptive in class, challenging rules and challenging a teacher's authority are also considered signs of masculine strength. These constructions are reinforced further where a boy's peer group also applauds such choices and behaviours, and so they may consequently refrain from showing to their peers any signs of applying themselves academically because of the fear of failing therein.

Indeed, for some boys, being disruptive in class is far easier and much more rewarding to them than applying themselves academically. Many of the hundreds of children excluded from school each year have learning difficulties and/or special educational needs. In this respect, it could be said that they have already failed in school. It is therefore unsurprising that boys with special educational needs are far more likely to be excluded from school than are higher or moderate learners. And, as mentioned earlier, of all those excluded, the large majority lose their school place for being violent, aggressive and disruptive.

In addition, it has been shown that the competitive school system further encourages "laddishness" among some boys (Jackson 2003). Consequently, some students are motivated to avoid failure by not participating at all (Covington and Teel 1996).

Many students will have witnessed the behaviour of some disruptive boys in classes and seen how it is much easier for them to achieve peer approval by mucking about, with aggression and laddishness, than it is to apply themselves academically. Laddishness is considered a defence, a self-worth protection strategy, to protect against accusations of failure, lack of ability and/or being seen as feminine. As some boys' identity is based on their masculine status, "laddishness" allows them to cope with the fear of academic failure by engaging in hegemonic masculine behaviours, which are accepted and admired within some masculine peer groups.

It is said that boys whose school attendance is poor are more likely than regular attenders to get involved in crime. Because of this, government policy encourages schools to keep problem pupils in school rather than excluding them. The disruption to other pupils' learning contributes towards making this policy ineffective, particularly if the male perpetrator finds learning difficult and gets little reward from education. If a boy believes in tough masculinity rather than educational achievement, then he may be more likely to choose laddishness, disruptive behaviour and possibly crime rather than education.

Doublethink and cognitive dissonance

Holding and believing in two or more beliefs which contradict each other may sound odd, but in examining the discussions of teenage boys and of school staff working with them, I have discovered that this is what regularly occurs. It is nonsense to suggest that men are naturally aggressive when there is evidence that shows that this is not true. It is also equally ridiculous to argue that some boys' behaviours in schools are problematic and then to argue that they are also normal. Promoting toughness, dominance and lack of empathy as desirable and normal attributes for boys and men is also a contradiction, particularly when we know that not all men subscribe to this behaviour and that such behaviour is not unique to men. Many of these behaviours are considered a problem in schools and wider society and, as such, are not valuable or desirable attributes. The continued investment in the "ideal man" ideology is an example of contradictory thinking.

Some years prior to the publication of "1984", George Orwell, although not referring to definitions of masculinity, defined such contradictory beliefs as "Doublethink" (Funder 2023). He described this as:

> "holding two contradictory beliefs in ones mind simultaneously, and accepting both", and significantly he added that it also included the need:
> "to forget any fact that has become inconvenient".

Sometime later, academic research similarly defined the holding of contradictory beliefs with incompatible values as "cognitive dissonance" (Festinger et al. 1955; Harari 2014).

I suggest that, in the interviews which follow, many of the contradictory beliefs and unsubstantiated opinions of adults and boys I interviewed can be determined as both "doublethink" and "cognitive dissonance". However, in continuing to hold and promote the contradictory values within the "ideal man" ideology, we are responsible for the continued promotion of the problematic male behaviours, which have been shown to cause considerable damage to some boys' education and contribute towards many of the damaging social issues discussed at the beginning of this book.

Contradictory thinking about this issue means that it cannot be resolved until people accept that the current desire and preference for boys to aspire to be the "ideal man" is halted. Men need to know that it is ok to act alternatively.

Summary and conclusion

In trying to understand the problematic masculine behaviours of boys at school, this last chapter has examined a range of literature, which suggests that much of boys' behaviour is closely related to their alignment within discourses of hegemonic masculinity. The literature illustrates how some boys who construct themselves within this dominant discourse may present behaviour that is judged to be disruptive, aggressive and alienated from education. They may also adopt "laddish" behaviours, distancing themselves further from education and learning. Through peer pressure, these behaviours are often normalised, encouraged, reinforced and exacerbated. Such behaviour potentially reinforces gender binary asymmetries, which further normalise hegemonic masculine behaviours and the belief in an "ideal man" to which all men should aspire.

What the examined literature fails to explore are the views and opinions of boys who display difficult behaviour or those of school staff working with problematic pupils. As this book is about "naughty boys", it seems pertinent to investigate the views of school staff and the views of those boys who have been excluded from school and have been deemed therefore to be "naughty".

To do this, a number of interviews were held with male pupils and school staff. These interviews revealed in particular how boys have to negotiate peer pressure in their attempts to understand what it means to be a man. The interviews also showed how normalised and engrained discourses of hegemonic masculinity are in the views and beliefs of staff (Banner 2015).

Note

1 [Frank Field was a well-known Labour Party politician who was the Member of Parliament for Birkenhead. He was a director of the CPAG from 1969 to 1979 and wrote for the pro-freedom of speech magazine *Standpoint*].

5

NARRATIVES OF NAUGHTY BOYS

This chapter is based on an analysis of notes and recorded interviews with boys. The analysis explores how boys constructed themselves within discourses of dominant masculinity. In addition, it also examines how boys drew upon various competing and incongruent discourses to understand, explain and justify a range of disruptive behaviours. During interviews with male students, all the young men referred to themselves and others as "boys", thus defining themselves as different from adult staff in schools. Therefore, I shall also use this construction to differentiate them from the school staff interviewed.

The pressures on boys to adhere to particular hegemonic masculine beliefs became very apparent right from the start. In the research carried out for this book, I spoke to boys who avoided subjects they thought feminine, such as reading, art and music, and opted for those activities they considered masculine, like sport, maths and science. However, their commitment to subjects and learning also varied greatly depending upon competition, their achievement and peer group pressure. In addition, choices and ideas about what subjects and activities are deemed masculine or feminine varied from one location to another. Rap music was considered good by some boys in one area I visited, whereas piano-playing was deemed inappropriate. One boy I spoke with never told anyone he played the guitar, while another boasted about playing the drums. Sport was also considered masculine, particularly football and rugby, because of the apparent links to fitness, toughness, competitiveness and aggression, whereas art was considered feminine and gay and was therefore to be avoided. The exception to this was graffiti art, perhaps because of its association with deviance and risk-taking. While it might be considered that both require artistic talent, some boys constructed one form of art as acceptable and superior to another. The question of how such constructions come to be requires some

DOI: 10.4324/9781003732785-6

investigation. Nevertheless, it is abundantly clear that bullying and peer pressure significantly influence some boys' attitudes and choices in school.

Behaviour, showing off and peer groups, normalising

As I have constructed excluded boys as naughty, I began my interviews by asking why they thought so many boys were excluded from school. Harry responded,

> Yeah, I think it's because with boys I think they like to show off in front of other boys sometimes, so, it kind of bigs yourself up if you do something like hurt someone.
>
> *(Harry, 16-year-old student)*

His explanation appears to draw on discourses to normalise male dominance and aggression. Harry constructs such behaviour as "showing off", designed to impress other boys, demonstrating to them that the actor is physically strong and able, thus "bigging himself up". Harry's brief extract is typical of many of the boys' explanations of disruption in class and their constructions of masculinity, with some constructing physical strength and aggression as necessary to demonstrate maleness to adults, peers and themselves. Many of the boys interviewed drew upon similar discourses, which constructed male strength and aggression as more important than other attributes or skills.

Like Harry, several boys used phrases such as "showing off" or "show off". Such acts of "showing off" and classroom disruption, while performed for other pupils, may also be performed as a challenge to teacher authority. Challenging teacher authority has two possible explanations. It may be a form of risk-taking, showing your peers that you are willing to risk reprimand or expulsion with your challenging act. It may also be a demonstration of masculinity, showing your peers that you are strong and brave enough to challenge authority. Whether it is a physical or verbal engagement, it illustrates how some boys may draw on discourses of normative aggression to reinforce a sense of self and to illustrate toughness to peers. The importance of a peer group is paramount in such a scenario.

Another boy, Fred, who, when asked to explain why so many boys are excluded, said:

JB: Quite a lot of boys get excluded don't they?
Fred: Yeah
JB: Why is that do you think?
Fred: Behaviour
JB: What sort of behaviour?
Fred: Disruptive stuff, fightin'. Spoiling the lesson 'n that.

JB: Oh, why do some people do that?
Fred: They like it or they get wound up 'n that.
JB: They like it?
Fred: Like spoiling it [lessons] and (pauses) You'll be like the show off in the class or something.
JB: The show off in the class?
Fred: So the others will think you're (hesitates) like, something.

In explaining why boys might engage in disruptive behaviour and spoil lessons, Fred's explanation draws on shared peer discourses to argue that disruptive and aggressive behaviour is enjoyed and performed to seek the approval of others, perhaps so that his peer group might construct the performer as tough and significant and therefore "something". Being "something" clearly means to be seen and constructed as important, masculine and tough in the eyes of one's peer group. Fred's apparently casual reference to what he constructs as disruptive behaviour seems to further strengthen how he normalises such aggression and to explain how it is used to "show off" and seek peer group approval. This resonates with Chambers et al.'s (2004) argument that there is considerable pressure from peers to engage and adopt hegemonic behaviours. Connell (2009) also warns that boys who avoid or depart from such "normalised" hegemonic behaviours often, as a result, themselves become the target for verbal and physical abuse. Thus, to avoid being a target, one has to "perform" particular forms of masculinity.

The power of one's peer group is immense for many boys. Concerns about this were further illustrated by Andy, who was asked to discuss his behaviour and exclusion from school.

JB: Is that the only time you've been excluded?
Andy: Ah, no once I punched someone in the mouth, they said something about my mum and I just got up out of my chair and give him a punch.
JB: They insulted your mum?
Andy: Yeah and that's how I reacted yeah.

The spontaneous yet casual manner in which Andy uses violence seems to show that he draws upon a dominant masculine discourse to construct such aggression as a legitimate response to taunts and insults. However, it may also be that he is responding to peer expectations about how men should respond to insults and therefore how he should defend his mum's reputation. This is clarified in the following extract.

Andy: . . . But, but some people just wind you up so they know you'll get in trouble.
JB: Oh, so your classmates irritate you?

Andy: Yeah, all the time, they can't control themselves or they wanna be show-offs in class.
JB: Why is that?
Andy: To be (pauses) I dunno, be top, standout or something.
JB: So whose fault is it when there's trouble in class?
Andy: Teachers. They need to sort it out and that.
JB: How can they do that?
Andy: (shrugs and frowns) It's their job.

When pressed further, Andy draws on a self-defence discourse to legitimise his behaviour, arguing that the other boy was taunting him. This may additionally illustrate that Andy believes, as Connell (2009) discusses, that he has been selected as a "target" for bullying or teasing by his peers. However, in a further move, Andy then legitimises teachers' authority and responsibility to handle pupil confrontation. Blaming the boy *and* the teacher further distances him from responsibility. However, while Andy attempts to legitimise his actions, it is clear that the only course of action apparent to him is to engage in violence, which suggests that he draws on a discourse of hegemonic masculinity in his understanding of how to behave in class and towards other pupils. This illustrates how imbedded hegemonic masculinity is within male discourse in school.

The peer group is also significant to Andy. Like Fred and Harry, Andy also used the "showing off" discourse to explain the reasoning behind some boys' disruptive behaviour in class. All three boys similarly argue that such behaviour is done to enhance peer positioning, with Harry saying it "bigs you up", Fred explaining they do it so others will "think you're something" and Andy suggesting they do it "to be top, standout, or something". All three explanations appear to relate to gendered acts of masculine disruption, aggression and violence that require a great deal of determination and effort to initiate and maintain, which is what the boys are discussing when they talk about "showing off" in order to prove manhood and impress peers.

While many boys appeared to want to normalise aggressive and defensive acts, peer pressure and peer friendships remained a significant feature in their discursive constructions. Much of this is illustrated in the following extract, where Roger, who had experienced frequent school moves, was talking about the difficulties of fitting in at a new school.

Roger: Obviously I'm not a quiet kid, I like to fit in and, but it didn't happen so (pause)
JB: Who do you like to fit in with?
Roger: Kids, mates.
JB: What sort of kids, the quiet ones?
Roger: That's hard, because I don't like quiet ones, cos I'm not a quiet lad, I like, like going out (pause) like doing stuff, not staying in, like all

day, playing XBox or somethink like that (pause) I like to get out and roam.

JB: Ok, so who do you think, if you were at school, you would mix with, would you mix with someone who is quiet and studious or somebody who wants to play football and . . . .

Roger: Yeah.

JB: What about fighting?

Roger: Nah, obviously I got out of that now I'm not a fighter but obviously if it comes to it and I'm self-defending myself I have to.

Although Roger draws on what might be determined as a masculine construction of interests and behaviours, he is also acknowledging the existence of alternative masculinities when constructing and then rejecting boys who are quiet and who might wish to stay in. Roger's comment, "I like to fit in", illustrates the importance he attaches to peer relationships and, as Mills (2001) says, being a "good mate". As discussed earlier, some boys draw on a repertoire of hegemonic masculine behaviours to impress their peer group. These behaviours may include fighting, risk-taking and other shows of aggression and toughness designed to fend off any suggestions that they lack masculinity (McGuffey and Rich 1999). It may be that this is what Roger is doing. Earlier in the interview, he had admitted that he did once engage in shows of aggressive masculinity, but now, he claims not to involve himself in fighting unless he has to. This indicates that, similar to Andy, Roger draws on an apparent self-defence discourse to defend himself not only from the aggressor wanting a fight but also from criticism and the threat of isolation from his peers should he not respond and defend himself as they expect. It also indicates that his response is to immediately draw on hegemonic masculine discourse, as his answer is to respond with aggression and violence. Drawing on hegemonic masculine discourse shows that he appears not to possess any alternative skills or an alternative discourse to draw upon. Masculine hegemony appears to be the dominant discourse.

His response also produces a question. What difference is there among defence, retaliatory action and bullying?

In this next example, Bob's construction of himself in a dominant masculine discourse is enveloped within references to threats from others and challenges to his reputation and thus, similar to Roger, links with discourses of peer pressure.

JB: Ok, so what were your fights about?

Bob: My fights were if someone basically disrespected me.

JB: Ok

Bob: (pause) or done something that I thought deserved a bang really.

JB: Ok

Bob: Obviously if someone's gonna hit you, someone's cussing you saying, oh yeah I bang your mum, I bang my mum, then you gotta show them that they can't really init, respect the way it is around here like. It's like your, your, rep is basically like, basically like when you go for a job interview you take your CV init.

JB: Yeah.

Bob: So that's how they know you, but for us kids we've got our rep basically like.

JB: You'll have to explain that to me, so what's rep?

Bob: Like reputation like, school, like when I was in Prince School, obviously like, I was one of the bigger boys that, like if I got one of the pussier boys saying like, yeah I bang him up, I bang him up then I got to tell him that he won't, I got to show him that he won't if he carries on saying that obviously cos I can't be going round school now, with people thinking that I'm a pussy when I'm not, so that's rep like you gotta tell em like.

Here, Bob aligns himself directly within discourses of dominant masculinity by constructing the need to use aggression, violence and sexualised vocabulary in response to what he considers threats and intimidation. Like Andy, Roger and Graham, Bob is concerned about what his peers might think of him. This he constructs as his "reputation", suggesting that his experience, skills and qualifications are constructed within his peer group by what he does and how he responds to taunts and jibes. The conversation with Bob suggests that his reputation has to be perpetually refined, defended and nurtured. Because of this, Bob is unable to ignore misogynist insults, such as being called a "pussy", or insults directed at his mother. To maintain his masculine reputation with his peer group, he has to regularly defend his masculine reputation and perform confident aggression.

The discourse of masculinity Bob utilises and the constructions Roger adopted later in his school life are subtly different from the "showing off" behaviours discussed earlier. They are engaging in what Butler (1993) defines as gendered performances. Bob's performance does not seem to be "showing off" because "showing off" appears to be linked with masculine acts designed to gain status, whereas Bob's actions are about maintaining an already established status within a volatile but established peer group. Marginally different, Roger is performing a construction where he has to be strong and able but only when he needs to defend himself against aggressors. While there appears to be a fine line between the earlier constructions of masculinity, the boys are engaged in performances that nevertheless reiterate a particular set of gendered norms, norms that are closely aliened with the "ideal man". The contrast between these boys' constructions of male behaviour is one of choice and contingency. Roger claimed that he might have to be aggressive to defend himself, while Harry and Fred maintained that boys choose to be aggressive to gain status. Bob alternatively suggested that it is necessary to defend an already established status. However, despite the choice available to participants, all these acts have the potential to further endorse aggressive behaviour as essential. Peer pressure is significant because the expectations of peers have the potential to further encourage and normalise aggressive behaviour, particularly if peers expect demonstrations of aggression and defence.

Reflecting the views of several boys interviewed, Bob said that there was considerable conflict between male students in schools. He was asked to elaborate:

> Yeah, cos you always get the people like, you got your popular people haven't you? And you got your stronger people. (pause) Then you got your "Geeks" and "Neeks" and stuff like that. Obviously like bullying and that goes on, like, obviously like, if there was no rules for fighting (pause) obviously, if you're getting bullied you're gonna whack them back.
>
> *(Bob, 16-year-old student)*[1]

Here, Bob draws on a taken-for-granted discourse to construct "popular" boys as having strength. He then draws on peer discourse to construct two alternative forms of masculinity, "Geeks and Neeks". These terms, "Geeks" and "Neeks", are reminiscent of the boys in the work of Martino (1999) and Willis (1978), where teenage boys created names for those whom they constructed as weak and different from themselves. Asked to explain these terms, Bob says:

> Well a Geek is obviously like, someone like, basically a Geek is a smart person, someone who chooses the right way basically and they're the ones who like get on with their work, they do their . . . they wanna get through school easy so they're doing, they're following the rules init. That's what we call a Geek.
>
> *(Bob, 16-year-old student)*

While Bob appears to construct himself within a normalising dominant masculinity discourse, contrarily, here, he draws on an alternative masculine discourse to construct "Geeks" as "smart" and choosing the "right way". This is in contrast to studies such as those of Martino (1999) and Francis (2009), who discuss how some boys marginalise and "other" boys who are considered to work hard at school. Bob's comments are also in contrast to "laddish" behaviours discussed earlier, where boys purposefully distance themselves from schoolwork. As Bob's recognition of "geeks" potentially undermines the discourse of dominant masculinity in which he ascribes himself, I asked him to elaborate further.

JB: OK, I'm gonna take you back to what you said just now, you said about the geeks are someone who is bright, yes, who does "the right thing" you said, what does that mean?
Bob: Like, gets on with their work, follows the rules and that.
JB: So is that the right way to be at school?
Bob: Well yeah, obviously, but thinking back to it now that should have been the way I was cos you know, I'm pretty fucked, I haven't got nothing now (Bob, 16-year-old student).

In clarifying what a "geek" is, Bob appears to be drawing on what Ball (2008) defines as a neoliberal discourse to construct himself as a failure because he had an unsuccessful school career, with no qualifications and few prospects. Consequently, the behaviours he is constructing as negative are dominant masculine behaviours, which moments before he was venerating and normalising. Such confused understanding, holding and valuing of two contradictory discourses appears to reflect "doublethink" (Funder 2023) or "cognitive dissonance" (Festinger et al. 1955; Arnold et al. 2009; Harari 2014), as discussed earlier.

Several of the boys interviewed made similar critical remarks about their past behaviours, constructing errors in these behaviours and recognising their resulting position. For example, towards the end of Horace's interview, I asked him, given the opportunity, what he would change in his life. He said:

> (Sigh), I would change how my mum (pause), if I could I would change it, I'd change how my mum brought me up, I'd change the environment that I was brought up in, I'd probably, I'd probably not want to be the guy who wanted to impress everyone and making people laugh and be the one who stood out. I'd rather just put my head down and work and actually achieve something. That's the only way you achieve something.
>
> *(Horace, 16-year-old)*

Similar to Bob, Horace also draws on a neoliberal discourse to condemn his own behaviour and to write himself off as a failure. The significance and power of peer groups are illustrated in the condemnation of his past need to impress his peer group by making them laugh. However, before he does this, Horace seems to mitigate his behaviour when he draws on a feckless single-mother discourse (Hey and Bradford 2006) to construct his mother's parenting skills as inadequate. He also briefly infers inequalities in his environment as contributory factors in his behaviour, too.

Boys who construct themselves within a dominant masculine discourse frequently insult or denigrate others to enhance their status and promote their particular constructions of themselves as men. In the interviews, this was often demonstrated during boys' discussions about boys they perceived either as inferior or who had challenged them and failed. Earlier, Bob had referred to "Geeks and Neeks". In explaining what a "Neek" is, Bob continues his derogation of those he considers weaker and inferior to him.

Bob: A Neek, a Neek is someone like basically someone that don't do what they're told and tries to, basically tries to be what they're not basically, that's a Neek, someone that, basically . . . a Neek is a Geek trying to be something he's not.

JB: So a bright kid who can work, but tries to be tough?

Bob: Yeah or like a bright kid that can get on with his work doing what he is trying to do like, basically, like, if he's a pussy like, a proper like fraggle, nothing like, he's a little minstrel basically trying to be something that he's not, like trying to tell everyone like oh yeah, yeah, that I'm this, I'm that, then obviously he's a Neek because he's not, he's not that person, and he's trying to be that person.

In this extract, Bob's tone appears to reflect anger and resentment. Unlike "Geeks", "Neeks" are to be despised because they are pretentious. Drawing upon a dominant masculine discourse, Bob abuses "Neeks" with misogynistic and other insults. Much of Bob's rhetoric relates to discourses of bullying and what Mills (2001) describes as "boundary policing" discussed earlier. It also illustrates the importance and superiority that Bob places on strength as a masculine attribute. Those who do not possess it are weak and inferior and are therefore to be despised.

Bob's commentary also demonstrates the normalising discursive techniques in which he appears to envelop aggressive and dominant masculine behaviour. He emphasises the obligation of his commitment when he says, "I got to show him . . . obviously". This may also illustrate the lack of choices available to Bob, particularly as he constructs himself as having failed at school. It would appear that his commitment and construction of himself within a dominant masculine discourse is all that is available to him. The use of "obviously" may be twofold, being directed at me, with the assumption that I (and all men) would unquestionably agree with him while also being used in an attempt to normalise his views to construct young men as naturally tough, aggressive and dominant.

While it has been shown that dominant masculine discourses appear to shape boys' initial discussions about behaviour, what has also been demonstrated is how, as conversations unfold, boys draw on a range of alternative discourses to explain, mitigate and distance themselves from responsibility for their behaviours leading to exclusion.

An example of this was given earlier by Andy, when he drew on discourse to construct teachers as responsible for dealing with conflict in school, saying, "Teachers. They need to sort it out. . . . It's their job". Distancing himself from his aggression, Andy blamed the teacher for not dealing with the situation in class. Although he does not say he would ask for teachers' help, his comment poses questions about how he might have reacted to the taunts from peers if the teacher had intervened earlier. Would a teacher's early intervention have enabled Andy to avoid using aggression and yet preserve his dignity and status in front of his peers? This is a huge conundrum because when other boys were asked if they would request the help of teachers to resolve conflict, many rejected the idea, in particular arguing that this would likely damage their reputation and peer position. This again emphasises how important a schoolboy's position within a peer group is.

In this next extract, I inadvertently ask Graham a leading question, which appears to direct him to talk about teachers that he did not like rather than discuss the helpfulness of staff. Despite this, Graham seems to indicate that he would not ask staff for help. He also draws upon an essentialist gender discourse, constructing boys and girls as naturally different.

JB: Graham tell me, you are not fond of teachers are you?
Graham: Teachers? No, not many. Take Mrs Stone. She picks on us. It's like, the people that are like, been horrible to her in the past, that's who she mainly picks on. Yeah.
JB: She picks on pupils who have been horrible to her?
Graham: Yeah. (pauses) No. She, she don't like kids and picks on them.
JB: I see. So you can't talk to her?
Graham: No, you're joking.
JB: Can you talk to any teachers?
Graham: (shrugs)
JB: Tell me Graham, what would your friends think, if you had a difficulty, would your friends think it was odd if you were telling the teachers?
Graham: (sighs and laughs) Yeah and if you done it too much they would probably rule you out like. Girls, they go to the teachers but (pause) nah.
JB: They would rule you out?
Graham: (inaudible) you'd be, like, (pause) They'd take the piss. Sorry I swore.
JB: It's ok.
Graham: Sorry.

While Graham indicates that he does not like this teacher and cannot talk to her, it is my question about what his friends might say that prompts him to draw on a discourse of peer disapproval. This extract is similar to several boys' comments about not engaging teachers to help with difficulties in school. All refuted the idea, stating that they had to independently defend themselves, presumably to maintain their masculine status within their peer group. Graham draws on a peer pressure discourse when he states, "They'd take the piss". As peer pressure and boundary policing are often exerted through verbal insults, Graham is acknowledging such pressures upon him to conform to discourses of dominant masculinity as defined and discussed earlier.

For Graham, the relationship with his class teacher is particularly relevant to his attitude towards her. In addition (and similar to Andy), peer pressure to conform within a dominant masculine norm also appears to contribute towards preventing Graham from asking a teacher for help. However, neither boy seems to dismiss the idea completely. It is possible that teacher intervention may offer the opportunity for peer pressure in the classroom to be lessened and consequently the related acts of masculine aggression to be minimised. The discourse of teachers as classroom disciplinarians and boys' constructions of their relationships with school staff will be explored further in the analysis which follows.

In contrast, in the following interview, John makes a different observation. Hoping to lead him into a conversation about peer pressure and relationships with teachers, I asked him:

JB: Can we talk about exclusion a bit more? How could exclusion be prevented?

John: I don't (pauses) it depends what people do I suppose.

JB: Yeah. Ok, like what?

John: I just think that you should stop and just think about what you're going to do and if you are going to do it, think about the consequences. If I had the chance to I'd go back and do it all again, I'd (pause)

JB: You'd what?

John: Just, do something different.

JB: Such as?

John: Just get through and get to college.

JB: College?

John: College, 'cause there, they (inaudible) they, respect you.

JB: Really?

John: Yeah you're like an adult, grown up. You can smoke and go out of the premises. Like go to Mac Donald's, you know, you know just do, be like an adult. It's not like school where you're, you're not, you're not (pauses) like you are like in a cage, like, although it's on this side of the fence rather than on the public side. You know in school, the (inaudible) is blocked off, like you got to be in the playground. Can't go where the trees, not allowed in the bike sheds and then, then (pauses)

JB: (Interrupts) So are you saying that you have more freedom at college or . . .

John: No I mean that you're an adult. You are treated with respect (pauses) not like here, or any school.

Initially, John appeared to be making the same fatalistic criticism of himself in the way that Bob and Horace did. He seemed to be drawing on discourses to construct his behaviour as incompatible with success in school. But his observations are problematic for him because he is wrestling with hegemonic discourses of masculinity while attempting to understand how a lack of education will impact his life in the future by preventing him from going to college.

However, when questioned further, he draws on alternative discourses to construct the school as prison-like. From a Foucauldian perspective, John discursively constructs school as a site of constant surveillance under a "normalising gaze", which is judging and examining his every behaviour (Foucault 1977). John's narrative highlights the disciplinary technologies which characterise a school, particularly those of regulation, containment and surveillance, and as such relate to the thinking of Foucault, who argued that factories, schools, barracks and hospitals all resemble prisons (Foucault 1977). Foucault's comparison of school with prison is particularly evident in John's account when he states he feels he is in a "cage". John also seems to object to the hierarchical positioning of himself as a child requiring adult containment. John sees going to college as the way to escape his imprisonment. Drawing on a popular peer discourse, he constructs college as a haven where he believes he will be allowed freedom and choice but will be treated with respect and as an adult. This poses the question that if schools were less rule-bound, would boys like John be able to perform masculinity differently? However, such a situation would seem to be in opposition to the views of other boys, who appear to be seeking additional support and discipline from teachers.

This examination of interviews with excluded boys supports much academic research, which argues that some boys' behaviours are constructed within discourses of dominant masculinity. It has been shown that a range of other discourses also has the potential to exacerbate and encourage boys' investments in dominant masculine discourses. Disciplinary technologies that characterise schools, teachers' classroom management, boys' home environment and parenting skills were also highlighted as contributing to boys' performances of masculine behaviours. However, while some interviewed boys attempted to normalise hegemonic masculine behaviours, they also offered a set of explanations which destabilise the construction of a single normalised, unitary masculinity. Some boys were able to be reflective, deconstructing their actions and setting them sensitively against the views and the behaviours of others, including teachers and "neeks and geeks". The willingness and ability of these boys to do this are much more complicated and nuanced than the way in which it is often portrayed, showing their awareness of the institutional constraints and norms by which behaviour is measured and socially constructed as normal.

Feminist theorists argue that dominant masculinity has been supported and justified through binary oppositions that give superiority to males over females. The boys' interviews certainly reflected this explanation, promoting aggression and apparently supporting peer-dominant discourses. The section which follows will explore the discourses boys drew upon as they attempted to explain and justify their constructions of such gender binaries.

Constructing and normalising essentialist gender discourses

In this section, I shall consider how boys discussed male and female behaviours and, in doing so, drew on particular discourses to reinscribe essentialist gender binaries.

> There's more violence in males though isn't there?
>
> *(Dan, 16-year-old student)*

Many boys echoed Dan's view above. As was discussed, some boys normalise male violence, strength and aggression by drawing on popular social and media discourses that contribute towards the construction of essentialist gender binaries. Dan did the same when asked to explain boys' aggressive behaviours further.

Dan: There's more violence in males though isn't there?
JB: Why's what?
Dan: I dunno, it's more masculine.
JB: What's that got to do with it?
Dan: I dunno (mutters) just the way boys think different to girls, don't they? (pauses for a moment and then laughs) Have you ever seen two girls in a boxing ring? (laughs) (Dan, 16-year-old student).

Dan's hesitation and use of the expression "I dunno" are employed twice, perhaps to give him the opportunity to think about how to respond, or possibly he assumes that the answer is obvious and therefore does not require explanation. His attitude and his answers, like those of many other interviewees, suggest that he may not have been previously asked to explain or defend such comments. Alternatively, it is also possible that my perhaps abrupt interview technique may have briefly disturbed him. However, he appears to recover and then draws further on taken-for-granted gender discourses such as those discussed earlier. Dan's simplistic defence is that boys and girls are naturally different, saying, "it's more masculine", and therefore requires no further explanation. However, when challenged further, he pauses again before drawing on an essentialist gender discourse, similar to the arguments put forward by Gurian (2001, 2005) and Sax (2005), who maintain that boys and girls think differently. It appears that Dan assumes this to be universally understood and may therefore expect me to agree when he adds the rhetorical question, "don't they?" As I do not respond, he attempts to defend this discourse further; his amused question is seemingly designed to denigrate females and thus prove his point: "Have you ever seen two girls in a boxing ring?" Dan, by saying this, appears to be ignoring day-to-day evidence of the ability of females to perform in sports historically dominated by men. He does this to defend his positioning within a dominant masculine discourse.

What Dan, and earlier Bob, illustrated is how misogynistic and sexual name-calling are used by males, not only to insult and denigrate females but also to attempt to reinforce discourses of dominant masculinity and strengthen and normalise gender binaries. In doing this, Dan firstly normalises violence, indicating that for boys to "underperform" in this context would be a sign of weakness. He then draws on an essentialist discourse to construct boys' and girls' thinking as naturally different, through which he constructs violence as something that boys do, but girls do not. He then reinforces this social construct with a misogynistic remark. As was discussed, Graham indicated his fear of underperforming, resulting in his friends "ruling him out" and/or "taking the piss". It seems that for boys like Dan, they will do all they can to avoid being constructed as weak and, in any sense, feminine. What they achieve is to highlight the fragility of such beliefs. However, many of the boys interviewed steadfastly maintained such essentialist differences.

Peter (whose interview was not recorded) said that he had been excluded from school "for fighting". When asked to explain why he had so many fights in school, he said that boys like him "got bored", whereas "girls did not". He made a particular point of emphasising that boys should be "tough and stand up for themselves" and were "weak" if they did not. Throughout the interview, Peter appeared to be drawing upon a simplistic essentialist discourse to characterise boys and girls as distinctly different, with boys being rebellious, aggressive and tough. It appears that Peter demonstrates such constructions of masculinity through performances of aggressive and confrontational behaviours, which have resulted in his exclusion from school.

Similar to Dan, when Bob was asked why more boys were excluded than girls, he immediately drew on a biological discourse, similar to neuropsychologists Baron-Cohen (2003) and Knickmeyer et al. (2005), to construct boys' and girls' behaviours as naturally different, an explanation that he uses throughout the following narrative.

> Because more boys, they've got testosterone and all that and boys all want to like, muck about, they always want to like just be like, they've got to show off more see, like, a girl if she's in a school, it's all about looks init, so they just have to look pretty, they don't care about that being naughty and that, but boys it's all about who's the funniest, who's the hardest, who's, who's got the most friends and most being like, most people like a funny person. If you're funny you're gonna have more friends that someone who's a moody prick really so, like, you try and be funny, you try and be the class clown and that, you get kicked out and you just don't get nowhere like that really, but that's the way it is in schools, that's the way kids are init. But with the girls, obviously they just have to look pretty, they don't have to act up they don't have to tell, they don't have to swear at the teachers and that, swearing at a teacher ain't gonna make their hair look any better is it?
>
> *(Bob, 16-year-old student)*

From this narrative, it is possible to put together a list of what Bob constructs as normal and necessary male behaviours and attributes. These range from being tough, naughty, popular and funny to being able to challenge a teacher's authority. "Showing off", discussed earlier, is also highlighted. Bob is flippant about girls, reinforcing essentialist gender binaries with his simplistic references to girls who "just have to look pretty". However, while demeaning girls, his comments also illustrate that Bob believes that boys are under significant pressure to perform a particular range of behaviours and significant performances for their peer group. He accepts this despite his acknowledgement that such behaviour leads to exclusion and a lack of achievement.

Such an acknowledgement indicates the strength of pressure on Bob to comply while also acknowledging that such behaviour is ultimately destructive. Significantly, he constructs masculinity as something boys have to do, but girls do not. Bob's narrative suggests that he feels he has little choice about how to behave, while girls are under no obligation to comply but are nevertheless constructed as weak and inferior. As has been discussed, peer pressure, together with possible peer teasing and bullying, has the potential to significantly encourage boys' engagement with performances of dominant masculinity. Fears of not being considered masculine, together with fears of being rejected and ridiculed by peers, contribute towards boys' exacerbating and normalising essentialist gender binaries and the associated dominant masculine discourses, which contribute towards boys' exclusion from school.

However, these gendered discourses are not necessarily stable. In the following narrative, Roger had been talking enthusiastically about boys' behaviour and fighting for some time. I asked him why he thought it was that more boys were excluded from school than girls.

JB: Ok, here's something that might interest you, more boys are excluded from school than girls, why is that?

Roger: I reckon one is cos boys always fight, boys can fight and girls can't (laughs).

JB: Or girls don't.

Roger: Yeah, girls don't (sigh). (Pause and silence)

JB: What about their attitude in lessons, I mean, you've been to lots of schools.

Roger: You see, you get, you get these stupid kids that are bored and then they like think, like, oh let's throw a pen at the teacher or the kids and, cos a girl won't do that she, like, she, I reckon if she ain't finished her work she'll go back to last lessons work or something like that (pause) but yeah (pause) I reckon that a kid will just get so bored they just do something to get excluded.

Similar to other boys, Roger begins by drawing on gender discourses, which construct boys' and girls' behaviours, thinking and abilities as naturally different. He does this when he laughs at the idea that girls could fight or be as aggressive and tough as boys. His commitment to the discourse that normalises male aggression and structures gender binaries is similar to that of Bob, Peter and Dan. However, when challenged, when I suggest that girls choose not to fight rather than being unable to, Roger hesitates, saying, "yeah" in apparent agreement; he then pauses before seemingly agreeing, "girls don't", and then, he falls silent. Although Roger may be accepting my correction, it may also be that my interview style may have contributed towards Roger's agreement by quelling his enthusiasm and reducing him to silence. To test this, I ask him a further question about pupils' attitudes in class. In response, Roger draws on a boredom discourse to construct the tedium of school contributing to "stupid" behaviour. He then, rather than insulting girls, praises their efforts and classroom abilities. This indicates that Roger sees reward in studious behaviour and the "waste" disruptive behaviour brings.

Although Roger appeared to construct boys' behaviour as superior and wanted to normalise and comply with essentialist gender binaries, he also shows hesitation and doubt in this belief. What Roger is describing in his narrative are his observations of dominant masculine behaviours among boys, behaviours that are endorsed and supported through peer pressures. Roger's hesitative reaction to my questioning may indicate the confusion and anxiety that accompanies those who attempt to negotiate competing and contradictory discourses (Harari 2014; Funder 2023).

While many boys also seemed to be attempting to construct and normalise gender binaries, one interviewee (while also promoting and normalising masculine dominance and male violence) suggested that girls also engaged in aggressive behaviours. These comments occurred during a discussion about the rivalry between secondary schools.

David: And all the schools, like most of the schools would not walk on the same side if they, if they think their school's got a problem like if they knew our school was after their school they would not walk on the same side of the road cos they would always jam outside the Red Brick Café init yeah on the benches yeah and there was a lot of them and almost all of them would walk across the other side which was a smaller pavement as well with the (pause).

JB: So there was a lot of rivalry then, between schools?

David: Yeah, but our school (pause).

JB: Amongst boys or girls?

David: Both, you'd see the girls having a good tear as well like, I remember yeah a girl called Lily she was like one of the fittest girls in my school in it yeah, this girl, black girl, come down to bang her up and she was mixed race init, the girl grabbed her yeah and threw her like that yeah and then, I can't remember, Lily did something init yeah and was like come on then yeah and then fucking the girl come at her and Lily grabbed her hair and started banging in her face in front of everyone.

David's response to Lily is interesting. It appears he is both amused and pleased by her behaviour, complimenting her by saying she is "fit", which presumably indicates that he considers her to be attractive and thus affirms that he is constructing Lily within a feminine discourse or, alternatively, he is not praising her for being feminine but because he admires her masculine characteristics in being able to physically assault another girl.

While he had previously been promoting, defending and normalising the uniqueness of aggressive behaviour as a male attribute here, in contradiction, he is now celebrating a girl who also behaves in an aggressive masculine manner. As such, David is describing what Halberstam (1998) and Paechter (2006a) define as "female masculinity". As David includes the compliment of feminine attractiveness, he is by default referring to what Francis (2010, 2012) refers to as gender heteroglossia, the coexistence of both femininity and masculinity. While the normalisation of aggressive male behaviours is accomplished by constructing it in opposition to femininity and by constructing it as something only men and boys do. David's illustration of and acceptance that girls can also perform masculinity inadvertently contradicts the normalisation of gender binaries, used to construct men as dominant, aggressive and violent and women as compliant, peaceful and passive.

This fragility of essentialist gender discourses is further illustrated in the interview with Horace. He began by accepting and normalising boys' aggression, but then, as the interview progressed, he drew on alternative discourses to make sense of gendered behaviours in school.

JB: So why aren't girls as violent as boys then?

Horace: Well, as the generations, as the generation's changes they are, they are getting a lot, lot, worse, the girls. But boys, they fight, boys have always learnt to fight, at young ages having a little fight. It's just what boys do really, boys will be boys, but (pauses).

JB: So it's natural?

Horace: It is sort of, it's, obviously I ain't saying it's like stabbing people and shooting people, cos that's not natural.

JB: Right.

Horace: But having a little, turn up with one of your friends because you never had a go on the football as many times as he did, it's just natural, because you're kids, you don't know hundred per cent, right from wrong and you just do it and that's why you learn from your mistakes and that's why life is about experiences, that's what life is, that's what makes life, a lot of experience that makes, life. So, girls they're a bit, I want pretty flowers and I want a nice (pause). As long as they got that then they're happy.

JB: (laughs) Right, ok. Were they born like that then?

Horace: I don't know, some boys are born more manish than men, you do get some women that are born very manly but then you get very lady, lady, very womanly, so I supp (pause).

Similar to other boys, Horace often appeared to want to normalise male aggression and construct boys and girls as essentially different. Initially, he seems to draw on a "historical norm" when he says, "boys, they fight, boys have always learnt to fight", but then, he challenges this logic. When asked to explain why he considers girls less violent than boys, he unexpectedly draws on a masculine–femininity discourse to argue that girls can be aggressive and that their behaviour is changing and becoming more aggressive. This supports David's views on female aggression. However, drawing on a historical discourse, Horace then disallows women from such behaviours by constructing aggression and fighting as something that boys have always done, normalising it with the proverbial "boys will be boys". While many of the boys interviewed constructed themselves as adults or were striving to become adults, here, Horace draws on a childhood developmental discourse (James and James 2004), describing it as a time of learning and thereby constructing the fighting boys engage in as part of their learning experience. However, the innocence that Horace constructs in relation to aggressive behaviours unwittingly aligns with academic debates, which construct dominant masculine behaviours as something learnt, rehearsed and performed and therefore not "natural".

Horace's reference to girls and flowers is a further example of how, by subjugating women, he is constructing masculinity in opposition to what he constructs as femininity. However, it appears that my questioning leads Horace to renegotiate the competing discourses about masculinity and particularly the gender binaries, which at times he appears to want to support and normalise. When I ask him, "Were they born like that?", he gives a very thorough explanation. Rather than drawing on gender binaries, he acknowledges the coexistence of a range of gendered performances, describing dominant masculinity, masculine femininity, feminine men and feminine women. Far from supporting essentialist gender binaries, Horace's narrative demonstrates a nuanced understanding of how identities are socially constructed. He also shows an understanding of how gendered identities are dependent upon the circumstances and particular social interactions at any given time.

Many of the boys interviewed attempted to normalise gender binaries, structuring their arguments upon hegemonic discourses, which authors such as Francis and Skelton (2001) have illustrated as fragile. During questioning, when these discourses were challenged, several of the boys resorted to humour and misogynistic comments in an attempt to support their claims. However, in the interview which follows, Graham's response is unexpectedly aggressive. While talking about differences between girls and boys, he joked about girls crying but then became angry when questioned further. This extract begins with a conversation about girls talking more than boys.

Graham:	No, no look. Girls talk more then boys, you know? They talk to the teachers and stuff.
JB:	What and boys don't?
Graham:	I don't. It's like I wouldn't go telling a teacher what has happened before that.
JB:	Why not, why wouldn't you?
Graham:	I don't like speaking to teachers like Mr Chalk. He's (pause)
JB:	Why what's wrong with him?
Graham:	He don't listen, he only sees what he sees, you know what I mean? And he's just (inaudible) rude. Talks down to you, like you're, you're, something.

JB: But can the girls talk to him?
Graham: They don't like him either. (laughs) They just ended up crying anyway.
JB: Boys don't cry?
Graham: You fucking (pauses).
JB: I'm sorry did I offend you?
Graham: That was a joke right?

It is not entirely clear why Graham responded to my comment as aggressively as he did. He may have found my interview technique offensive. Alternatively, he may have misunderstood my remark, which was not directed at him but was a counter to his suggestion that girls cry but boys do not. While the reasoning behind Graham's behaviour is unclear, what this extract appears to indicate is how sensitive and significant it is for boys like Graham to position themselves within a unitary construction of masculinity. As indicated by Horace, they appear to do this by drawing on a particular discourse to normalise gender differences, thus constructing masculinity, as Francis (2000) argues, in opposition to femininity.

This analysis of interviews with boys indicated the fragility of the gender binary discourse. What is particularly striking is how boys, despite showing the instability of this discourse and illustrating an understanding of gender heteroglossia, continued to draw on discourses of gender binaries in order to try to defend and countenance their dominant masculine behaviours. They did so despite the contradictory discourses they inadvertently illustrate that they are aware of. Some boys seem to understand that there is a range of masculinities and femininities and that these are not exclusive to boys/men or girls/women. While my questioning may have caused some boys to renegotiate their thinking, the pressure and power afforded to peer discourses, constructions of gender binaries and dominant masculine discourses seemingly draw them back and away from alternative constructions.

Naughty boys and parenting discourses

In this section, I shall be looking at the reasons boys gave for their behaviour at school, their subsequent exclusion and then how they included and implicated parents in their accounts. Although almost all boys interviewed constructed aggressive behaviour as normal for males, when conversations took an autobiographical tone, they often supplemented this discourse by drawing upon other contributory factors. In particular, the behaviour of adult figures and parents in the home was frequently referred to, with several boys drawing upon and merging popular role model and parenting discourses to validate their claims.

During discussions with Horace about his home life when he was younger, he described his mother's boyfriend as a role model, saying,

Horace: He's just a poor excuse for a human being and I had to live with him, I had to (pause) have him as a role model, what couldn't role model a dog.

JB: Why do you say he was a poor role model?

Horace: He never worked, he never went to school when he was young. He was in care and all that sort of stuff. He's a gambler, he takes drugs, he, he don't do nothing for the house, he wouldn't put food in the fridge, he wouldn't paint a wall, he wouldn't put carpet down, he wouldn't do nothing, he'd just sit round, smoke fags, leave ash on the floor, live like a slob (Horace, 16 year old student).

Now 16 years old, Horace constructs this man's behaviours as unacceptable, suggesting that when he was younger, he was the only example available to him and thus referred to him as a role model. In addition, his critical description draws on a working-class patriarchal discourse in which the father is both provider and maintainer of the home. He begins this next extract by talking about his mother's drug and alcohol abuse.

Horace: Well there's, she's obviously, she, she was in the wrong place at the wrong time and when I was living at home, she wouldn't care, for not going, for not going to school (pause) but err, she blames that, err her addictions started over being raped, she says she got raped and she was, not saying I disbelieve her, obviously, but she says she got raped when she was about 9, something like that and that's when she started alcohol she never told me when I was younger, she only told me when I was getting older, to know, what I wanna know is why, why she was such a crap mum to be honest, that's I wanted to know the answers, but obviously she got raped then and she started drinking to, to deal with it, to push the problems, she didn't tell none of the family and she had to deal with the situation on her own, so she started drinking and one thing led to another and she started taking drugs she started drinking (inaudible) she just, the ball out of the cycle hasn't stopped and it just got worse and worse and her health has decreased constantly.

JB: And when you were a child living with this, what did you think?

Horace: (pause) well living with it, because I was brought up with it, it was err, the norm. Getting brought up with it was just, the just,

> the norm it was just, it was just, it was just what you do it weren't nothing out of the ordinary . . .

Here, Horace considers his upbringing through a normalising middle-class lens to draw on a poor parenting discourse, similar to Scott et al. (2010) and Lopez et al. (2008), who construct a correlative relationship between parenting skills and children's behaviours discussed earlier. Significantly, there is a very distinct contrast between Horace's construction of his mother and her partner. Horace refers to his mother as "a crap mum" but moderates this by drawing on a child abuse discourse to explain that her parenting ability was affected by abuse and her subsequent dependence on alcohol and drugs. In contrast, he is highly critical of his mother's partner, even though it is apparent that he also abuses drugs and alcohol. It may be that Horace is simply using his mother's boyfriend as a scapegoat for his family's situation and his attitude towards school and subsequent exclusion. However, there is an alternative view. In criticising his mother's partner, he continues to draw on a working-class patriarchal discourse and lists a range of responsibilities that he constructs as indicators of an effective father and husband. Further, in drawing on this discourse and excusing his mother, Horace is both constructing men as dominant and women as weak and dependent. Thus, Horace is releasing his mother from responsibility, but, in doing so, he appears to also be dismissing the possible influences of his mother's parenting and behaviour. His final comments are also pertinent. When asked what he had thought about his home life, he drew on a discourse of childhood innocence. This further constructs his mother and partner as inadequate and therefore responsible for his behaviour. Overall, the events during Horace's childhood, while clearly damaging, appear to have reinforced discourses of gender binaries and in particular further reinforced ideas of patriarchal masculine dominance.

In an earlier conversation with Horace, he discussed how, when he was younger, he had not been able to concentrate or comply with rules and authority at school, but now, at 16, he wishes that he had. He also constructed these shortcomings to his upbringing at school, saying:

> I was quite a naughty child, I weren't, I weren't, weren't very well behaved, my upbringing weren't very good, more dragged up than brought up . . . I never had a, never had a stable environment, I weren't, I never had a routine, I never had no structure it was just all by ear and everything went by ear and what would happen tomorrow, I dunno (pause) I'm still confused in what happened today (pause) so I just, I just, I didn't know what I was doing from tomorrow, basically. I didn't know if I was going to school,

> I didn't know if I was going to stay at someone, random's house, I didn't know what I was doing, so going to school was just like a playground, if you see what I'm saying, that it err, never really, just showed me a lot of kids and because I was missing days here and I was missing days there, obviously it weren't my fault cos obviously I wasn't old enough to take myself to school, but I was missing days here, I was missing days there I was behind.
>
> *(Horace, 16-year-old student)*[2]

Horace begins by blaming himself, drawing on what Timimi (2005) might determine a "naughty boy discourse". Although constructing himself as "naughty", he then adds that he was "dragged up", not "brought up". These expressions appear to have been drawn from routine public discourses that habitually pathologise working-class parents, constructing them as lazy, negligent and inadequate, an issue debated by Titus (2004) and Westwood (1996). Horace's comments also reflect the middle-class discourse of "poor parenting" or "adverse parenting" discussed by Liabo and Richardson (2007). Such issues were discussed earlier. By drawing on these discourses, Horace further positions his mother and her partner as responsible for his behaviours and achievements.

It is significant that although in this conversation with Horace he criticised his stepfather, he does not openly condemn his violence; instead, he referred to him as "a slob", criticising his cleanliness, lack of DIY skills, gambling, drug-taking and work ethic. Earlier in the interview, he had said:

> my mum . . . she was constantly having arguments and fights, with her boyfriend, well me being, (pause) I dunno not a mummy's boy, but I do love my mum, like there's no tomorrow, so I'd always stick up for her even if she was in the wrong, so I'd always end up fighting him. Like I was only what, 10, 11 and I was fighting and trying, but he'd fight back cos I was, I was a big boy and I would have to hit him or something, so it was quite a rough house to be honest.
>
> *(Horace, 16-year-old student)*

Throughout Horace's narrative, he is drawing on multiple and competing discourses as he attempts to explain and make sense of his educational experiences and his relationships with his mother and her partner. In this extract, seemingly in an attempt to protect his mother from criticism, Horace attributes the blame for the violence in the home to his mother's boyfriend. However, although condemning his mother's partner in many ways, he does not condemn the aggression and violence displayed by himself or by her. This appears to reaffirm his commitment to a discourse of normalised aggression, constructing violence as a useful and valid resource. Horace combines this with an apparent commitment to the dominant male discourse. Reinforcing his construction of himself within this discourse, he states that he was a "big boy", not small and inferior, and therefore not weak. In doing so, it seems he is further affirming the superiority and normality of his own aggression and physical strength. Following this, Horace hesitates when he says that he loves his mother, possibly viewing this as an admission of weakness. He may see potential in the accusation of being "a mummy's boy" as a challenge to his own masculinity and so adds that, even though he was young, he could fight a grown man. So, while Horace constructs and condemns particular male behaviours as being detrimental to his own development and behaviour, contrarily, he gives the impression of defending the dominant masculine discourse, promoting male aggression and strength as normal while rejecting personal misogynist insults such as "mummy's boy".

Horace's narrative illustrates how the power of one discourse can overwhelm that of another. His experiences and the range of discourses to which he seems to align appear to reinstate and strengthen the already powerful discourse of masculinity, a discourse that limits the options available to Horace and eliminates the possibility of him "doing" masculinity differently. Horace invests in a range of discourses at various moments to make sense of his educational experiences, his upbringing and his relationships with his parents. In doing so, he is attempting to determine some truths. This illustrates, as Foucault (1980) explains, how people produce truths within discourses. However, the efficacy of Horace's truths is undermined because, as he seeks to explain and apportion blame, he holds on to contradictory and outmoded discourses of aggression, patriarchal dominant masculinity and gender binaries, which are at odds with middle-class constructions of parenting skills, behaviour and school achievement.

Horace was not the only boy to attempt to form links with various parenting and role model discourses. In the following interview, Harry began by discussing bullying and school uniforms. This then moved on to statements about the home influencing a pupil's behaviour at school.

Harry: . . . there are a lot of kids who maybe don't have the privilege of some other kids of the money they get and the clothes they wear, they might wear the same clothes for a couple of days in a row and people would embarrass some people who would take the mick out of that.

JB: Yeah.

Harry: That's not, you can't help that, it's like (pauses)

JB: Because you haven't got a lot of money and so on?
Harry: Yeah it's not their fault it just makes them a target really for people to pick on.
JB: Right, is that kids who come from homes that don't have a lot of money, does that cause other problems as well for them?
Harry: Yeah I think a lot of, they've got a lot of stuff, if they've got problems at home I think it's all inside, like all keep inside and not telling anyone, coming to school and release their anger in ways that you shouldn't.
JB: What sort of things?
Harry: Like lashing out or something, to someone who's not even being that bad to them, not being horrible to them, they end up saying stuff that they regret or hit and that is one of the reasons they get excluded as well.
JB: What's happening at home that's causing that?
Harry: Well it could be, there's loads of stuff that could happen, it could be like, your parents hit you, or they (pause) smoke drugs or there's they just neglect, they don't look after you the way they should, they don't feed you the nutrition you should have or anything. So it, it's not a very good way to be brought up and it could lead you like in the wrong direction. Because when you are at home you're not seeing any good role models really, aspiring to be like . . .

Harry began this conversation drawing on a poverty discourse to argue that being poor can result in teasing and becoming a possible target for bullying at school. This concurs with observations of Ball (2008) discussed earlier. When asked if such poverty might cause other problems at school, Harry abruptly moved his conversation on, seemingly drawing on a parenting discourse to construct pupils' difficulties and exclusion from school as being caused by problems in the home. Harry's argument is somewhat different from that of Horace. Horace said his upbringing did not equip him for school. Harry argued that problems at home might result in outbursts of anger, which may lead to exclusion. Harry also loosely used the term "neglect", an expression used by Rutter and Smith (1995) and others who draw links between constructions of parental neglect and educational failure.

Despite the subtle differences in the two boys' versions of their experiences, both seem to be drawing upon a normalising parenting discourse similar to that which appears in the media. Assarsson and Aarsand (2011) argue that this construction of parenting takes no account of cultural diversity or social inequalities, such as poverty. By drawing on this discourse, Horace and Harry classify and condemn, constructing particular poor working-class parents as responsible for their children's behaviour and exclusion from school, despite the inequalities that accompany poverty and the assumptions of truth contained within this discourse.

Earlier, the work of Merton (1957, 1986) was discussed, and consideration was given to his particular role model hypothesis. Both boys draw on the popular and simplistic role model discourse, with Harry in particular arguing that parents should be role models and inspire their children and that where they do not, problem behaviour may result. In contrast to Merton, Horace argues that where there are no alternatives, then the only available adult will be copied regardless of the quality of their behaviours and thus will become a role model by default. Using these intersecting discourses, both boys appear to be further pathologising working-class parents, and, in doing so, they construct them as responsible for some boys' difficult behaviours at school, behaviours which are influenced by discourses of hegemonic masculinity.

The parenting skills discourse also featured in other boys' narratives. Similar to Horace, Peter (whose interview was not recorded) briefly discussed this in relation to his ability to concentrate at school. He said that he often truanted from school because he got bored. He was asked what his mother thought of his truanting, and he appeared dismissive, shrugging and not answering. However, without prompting, a moment later, he added that he could not concentrate in school when there were lots of children about. When I asked why this was, he said that he often worried about his family at home in case they were in danger. He then added that he needed to be part-time at school so that he could go home and check on them.

This appears to relate to Harry's earlier comments about children having problems at home and keeping it "all inside". What Peter appeared to indicate is that things happened at home that so disturbed him that he was worried and unable to concentrate at school. Further questioning did not reveal what it was that worried Peter so much. However, earlier he had talked about fighting and being tough and felt that this was acceptable and normal, saying that boys should stand up for themselves and were weak if they did not. Although Peter's interview was short and not electronically recorded, the information gathered implies a boy who draws upon a dominant masculine discourse and who also constructs himself as responsible for his family. This is in contrast to the Western social construction of childhood that views children as dependent on parents, a matter variously discussed by Timimi (2005), Katz et al. (2007) and Uprichard (2008).

The discourse of parenting was also illustrated in the interview with David. Much of David's interview was dominated by his discussion about fighting, aggression and defending himself. When I asked him if he could remember when he was very young, he continued to discuss his aggression and fighting, but then he gradually shifted to reminiscing about his early childhood.

JB: Ok, now the last bit, do you remember when you were very young (pause) very, very young?

David: Yeah some, some bits of my life.

JB: Ok what was life like?

David: (Pause) well it was kinda hard, to be honest, like cos mum was by herself init yeah, my dad had fucked off and like, like there was like even, even, first school for me yeah like cos I remember them years quite well yeah (pause).

JB: Mmm Mmm.

David: Like I got into like two fights in the whole of the first school yeah, which is three years and that was it yeah and then it just, as everyone got older it just escalated init like, but when I was young, even before that nursery or reception like first even two fights apart from that, that was nothing out of all those terms init.

JB: Mmm mmm.

David: And like I, I . . . got more violent init but it was the only way that I was gonna show people that, I'm not a prick like that, cos people these days are like you back down the first time and say, I can't be arsed yeah, those do it again, that's the thing so but I remember back in the, I used to be a good kid (laugh) when I was very young, like when I was in nursery yeah I remember yeah the first day I went there yeah, I didn't want to go there init and I went there and I was behaving and I used to help out tidy up and things like that.

JB: Mmm and you can remember that?

David: I remember as well this one day yeah, like I don't know how I managed to remember it yeah, even my mum turned round and remembered it yeah, I remember yeah when I was living with my mum ages and ages before . . . like there was this one picture that I cut out and it was a cat init, a tabby cat init and um, like it was a proper photo init (pause).

JB: Mmm, Mmm

David: They must have taken in it and brought it in and they were letting kids cut them up and things. I remember I touched it one day yeah like I was looking at all my shelf, like I used to have bookshelves in a row and like there were flowers on top yeah like fake ones from when I was born yeah.

JB: Yeah.

David: And I saw this photo and I picked it up init yeah and I looked at it I couldn't remember where I got it and later on a had a dream that I remembered actually cutting up I remember the teacher when we sat down on the floor and she was like um, she was like, so what has everyone been doing today, has everyone been doing that yeah, then like we were like yeah we been doing cutting and all this yeah and I went out I wasn't sure if that actually happened yeah that it was a bit weird that dreamt about it and I thought, I went and asked my mum and she goes yeah cos that was, that was my first day of being there before she come to pick me up and she saw me doing that.

JB: And is that a nice memory?

David: Yeah, I still remember that one.

JB: Did your mum do things like that, cutting out?

David: Not really, she, to be honest, mum didn't really have enough time for like me mainly like.

JB: Why not?

David: Cos I was the one always getting into trouble and things like that, like I'm basically like the black sheep of the family init . . .

This extract appears to confirm David's alignment with dominant masculinity and his construction of the need for boys to display aggressive defensive behaviours. Similar to other boys, this narrative also shows that David draws upon a Western social construction of childhood and parenting, constructing children as vulnerable and dependent upon their parents. In addition, and similar to Horace, David also appears to draw on a patriarchal parenting discourse, constructing a specific, irreplaceable role for fathers with their sons. David illustrates this through sympathy for his mother, who was left alone to raise the family when his father left. Such discourse has the potential to further enforce constructions of gender binaries, particularly for those who construct specific parenting roles for mothers and fathers while also constructing women as weak and inferior to men. Such constructions appear to compound David's resentment of his father, which is illustrated by his use of aggressive vocabulary, such as that used when he explains that his father "fucked off".

While David appears to maintain his construction of himself within a dominant masculine discourse and an alignment with a gender binary discourse, in contrast, he also appears to briefly discuss what Francis (2012) refers to as male femininity. This is illustrated when David recollects early memories of cutting out a picture of a cat, which is placed on a shelf in his room with some flowers. Reflecting on the incident, David is calm and apparently content at engaging in what might be constructed as a feminine activity and thus in opposition to what Mills (2001) describes as "images of the 'ideal man'". David's narrative is in contrast to that of Horace, who earlier used comments about flowers as a means of belittling girls and thus demeaning feminine activities.

While much of David's narrative is dominated by his construction of himself as tough and masculine, here, he refers to a brief period in his life when he was "good", thus potentially accepting and further constructing his fighting and current behaviours as "bad". This section of David's narrative appears to show that he has some understanding of alternative masculinities and is also able to align and construct himself within such alternative feminine/masculine discourse; however, briefly, he does so. Together with constructing himself as "bad", this suggests that David is also able to align with discourses which construct dominant masculinity as problematic.

The narrative of both Horace and David indicates that while constructing some of their behaviour at school as inappropriate and blaming themselves for it, they also draw on popular parenting discourses to construct mothers, but particularly fathers, as responsible for providing appropriate guidance and support to children. Mayer (2001) and Scott et al. (2010) similarly construct the need for particular skills to be nurtured at home by parents. Additionally, academic, political and media discourses often construct absent fathers and single mothers as irresponsible and unskilled at caring for their children. While Horace and David appear to do the same, their criticisms are constructed by drawing on a working-class patriarchal discourse, enabling blame to be placed on absent fathers or stepfathers rather than mothers. The boys' continued construction of dominant masculinity and gender binary oppositions supports their construction of working-class patriarchy, which in turn enables them to both criticise and mitigate what they construct as their mothers' inadequate parenting skills.

In my interviews with boys at school, they overwhelmingly thought that smacking a child was not only justifiable but also essential. There is indeed much media support for physical punishment, with comments such as, "it never did me any harm". This is despite the fact that smacking a child is now banned in the United Kingdom (Ritchie 1989; Timimi 2005; Minogue 2009). However, it is widely believed that violence may be further encouraged by such discipline methods and therefore shows how parenting has the potential to influence a pupil's behaviour at school, particularly if a young person believes that smacking is an acceptable way to deal with behaviour that one does not like.

Like many adults, the boys claimed that being physically punished persuaded a child not to repeat the unacceptable behaviour that they had performed. One boy said:

> Well obviously I was brought up with that sort of discipline, you be naughty, you get a smack on the bum, like that's what you deserve, basically if you tell a kid off (pause) it's no consequences just a telling off that's it, if you get a slap then your gonna know next time not to do it, cos your gonna get another slap.

While advocating that physical punishment was effective, this young man also added that just being "told off", or what we might refer to as discussion and negotiation, was not as effective as a means of correcting a child's poor behaviour.

Further to this, academic work argues that one of the major reasons for confrontation in schools with boys is that schools are organised around middle-class ideals and values, which include negotiation and non-violence. As such, these values are at odds with some working-class families and some boys who consider such methods as non-masculine. We can see how particular parenting methods such as physical punishment may also contribute towards conflict with teachers and ultimately exclusion. As discussed, contained within this disciplinary regime is a contradictory structure about how boys/men should respond towards authority (Lareau 2003; Peal 2014). If, as is suggested, most teachers rely on negotiation and non-punitive methods to deal with discipline, then such middle-class approaches may be at odds with some boys' constructions of discipline, particularly those who believe that men should act aggressively to confront problems.

Various UK government reports emphasise the importance of the involvement and responsibility of parents in their children's behaviour in school and have frequently demonised and blamed the parents of children whose behaviour falls below that deemed adequate (Mayer 2001; Scott et al. 2010).

As has been discussed, boys dominate the statistics around problematic behaviour in schools, in particular for the use of physical aggression and their involvement in fighting. Yet, in apparent contradiction, being able to fight and defend oneself is considered by some parents as a desirable male characteristic. In relation to this, when a boy does not cooperate and behave as the school desires, it is not uncommon for parents to be blamed for their son's apparent misdemeanours (DCSF 2007b; Harris and Goodall 2007).

Boys' behaviour and teachers

> It's not all down to students. It's how teachers deal with it.
>
> (Andy, 16-year-old student)

While boys discussed parents and parenting, they also implicated teachers in causing or exacerbating boys' difficult behaviours at school, as suggested by Andy in the quote above. This will be the focus of this section. Earlier, Harry had mentioned bullying in schools; the following interviews expand upon this discussion.

It is significant that the next three interviewees, Terry, Sid and Peter, refused to have their conversations recorded. All had a statement of special educational needs based on their problematic behaviours and had previously been temporarily excluded for aggression towards staff and other pupils. The three boys voiced similar concerns about bullying and the lack of action teachers took to deal with it. While it might be supposed that because of their aggression, these boys construct themselves within a hegemonic masculine discourse, they all claimed that they had to defend themselves because they were bullied, and no action was taken by school staff. They had been allowed to return to school but were aware and fearful that any further acts of violence might lead to their permanent exclusion.

The boys' refusal to have their interview electronically recorded, together with their willingness and keenness to be back in school, indicates that they acknowledge and draw not only on a discourse that values education but also on a discourse of hierarchical positioning between staff and themselves. They also acknowledge the power afforded to the school as the "institution of correction" and the "normalising gaze" to which they are subjected (Foucault 1977). While such scrutiny leads to the boys' compliance and self-regulation, it is also accompanied by anxiety and distrust, possibly exacerbated by the teacher seated in the corner of the room throughout the interviews. Explaining to me that they were bullied in school, all three boys drew on a discourse of teacher responsibility, manifested in the need for staff to care and intervene in pupil confrontation. This construction is similar to Andy's comments, which were aggressive to a pupil when the teacher did not intervene on his behalf. Like previous interviewees, who construct parents as having responsibilities to care for and nurture their children, these boys also seem to have expectations that teachers should care for them in school.

While the boys accepted their subordinate place in the hierarchical positioning of power, they also seem to have developed distrust structured around the repressive discourse of school discipline, which did not allow them to defend themselves. Maintaining a passive, compliant position is the challenge for these boys. While they are under the constant scrutiny of teachers, so too, it seems, are teachers by students. The boys construct teachers as having responsibilities to care for them. If they fail, then the behavioural discourse the boys attempt to adhere to may again be discarded as they then draw on an alternative discourse of defensive hegemonic masculinity to protect themselves against bullies and the perceived inaction of teachers.

This tension between boys and teachers is further illustrated through the following interview with Graham.

Graham: No, like (pause) um I got um, threw a chair at a teacher once but (pause)

JB: Why was that?

Graham: Just the way they were talking to me and treating me and I didn't like it.

JB: Can you explain?

Graham: Like I said, they, they talk rude to you and then when you're rude back they don't like it and then there's trouble and you get excluded.

JB: What do you mean by rude?

Graham: They, they look down on you, you know (pauses) They talk to you like you're some, some, I dunno, like you're below (pauses) small, nothing and that's rude, like you're nothing. Like, they say, "Oi Smith", they don't say, "Graham or please, excuse me", they just shout rude at you. If you don't say Mr or Mrs then, then they're, wow! (pauses) S'not right.

While Graham's behaviour may be constructed within a hegemonic masculine discourse, it is further explained within Foucault's description of the disciplinary techniques in operation in institutions such as schools. Foucault argues that the acceptance of discipline brings into play the "subordination of one group of people by another" (Foucault 1977). Unlike the three boys above, it appears that Graham is unwilling to be subjected to such subordination. Drawing on a discourse of mutual respect, he constructs the teacher's attitude towards him to be disrespectful. His construction of himself within a hegemonic masculine discourse is further at odds with his construction of the teacher as rude, demanding an aggressive masculine response to show the teacher and his peers that he will not be treated disrespectfully.

David's reaction is similar to Graham's.

JB: So what was the problem with the teacher?

David: I can't even, I can't, like his name was Mr Christie init and he like was boying me off one time init, like, he tried like . . .

JB: What does that mean, boying you off?

David: Tried to make me look small init.

To explain the teacher's rudeness, David chooses the expression "boying me off". While this might be understood as a generic expression of belittlement, it also suggests being referred to as an immature child or, more specifically, a boy rather than a man. The teacher concerned might draw on a discourse of the undeveloped child, as explained by Cannella (1997), defining children as lacking and therefore requiring adult intervention. David objects to such a construction, considering it to be an insult designed to ridicule him because it constructs him as childish and unmanly. As discussed, masculinity is defined by what it is not, and David and other boys consider themselves neither childish nor unmanly. Therefore, being constructed as a boy undermines the discourse of hegemonic masculinity associated with manhood in which they invest so heavily.

This is an interesting objection, at odds with boys' previous constructions. At the beginning of this chapter, I noted that most male student interviewees constructed themselves as boys, thus distancing themselves from adult school staff. Following this, several boys, including David, drew on parenting discourses to discuss parenting skills and responsibilities. In making such constructions, they appear also to be drawing on an essentialist discourse to construct childhood as real, where children are constructed as vulnerable and dependent upon adults. However, it appears that teacher references to childhood are considered by some boys as demeaning and insulting, particularly when used for the subjugation and disciplining of pupils. Such an act is demasculinising, particularly when enacted in the presence of peer groups, and as such encourages aggressive and violent responses.

Concern about teachers' discipline skills was raised by other boys who thought that teachers should be more sensitive and proactive in handling incidents and behaviours in school. In the following narrative, Andy discusses this and refers to himself as a student, distancing himself from child-like constructions associated with boys.

JB: How could exclusion be prevented?

Andy: (Yawns and stretches) It's not all down to students. It's how teachers deal with it. Like, like, what they do to get a student to calm down and that. Or, or if they have wound you up in the first place.

JB: Really?

Andy: Because nine times out of ten it's not the actual thing event that gets you excluded it's how you talk to the teacher after, because you're that wound up, (pause) they don't like help you calm down, you're just like, er, don't want to talk to you right now and that's usually what gets you excluded because it all builds up if you know what I mean?

(Stands up). I think the best way to prevent something is do actions before it actually happens say like, if your getting wound up by the teachers and that, if you just go to someone and say look I'm not going into that class, she's gonna wind me up, I'm gonna get excluded. (Pushes his chair in and makes to leave)

JB: Thank you very much Andy for your time.

Andy: Yeah, thanks. (hesitates) Sorry I gotta meet someone. But you know (pauses) One thing they do is, my mum used to like, when my mum had been rang up by teachers saying like what I've done and that, because my mum knew I had a short temper and she would be like, all the teachers knew I had a short temper but they still like, they make it sound ten times worse than what it is, like, he started it, we've done this, we've done that,

	we've said this and this is how you have not finished it, but it's never (pauses and opens door).
JB:	Thank you Andy
Andy:	Brilliant. (leaves room)

While it might appear that Andy's narrative is but a simple criticism of a teacher's handling of a confrontation between two pupils, it suggests more than this. Like David, Andy draws on discourses of masculinity and adulthood to construct himself as an independent adult male requiring minimal adult support. This is further supported by Andy's construction of himself as a student, not a boy. He also draws on affectivity discourses to normalise anger and legitimise his right to express irritation at someone else's actions. However, the authority of the teacher undermines his discursive constructions. Similar to other boys, Andy objects to the power afforded to teachers, their scrutinising disciplinary gaze and their construction of students as children. Andy particularly objects to the lack of autonomy offered by the childhood innocence discourse because this prohibits him from being an adult and denies him freedom to deal with conflict, his anger and his emotions. Andy further objects to teachers' hierarchical positioning, enabling them to observe and criticise students and report their judgements to parents. Such power further enforces the socially constructed binaries of student and teacher and of adult and child, to which Andy and some other boys object. What remains throughout is Andy's alignment with masculine aggression and his right to use this where he deems appropriate.

Not all boys were critical of teachers. In this next extract, Horace compliments teachers who have been patient and have helped him with his aggressive and violent behaviour in school. He explained:

	I've had quite a strong bond with a few teachers throughout the years with my schooling, mainly in a weird way, the head, the main, the main person in a way because, well primary school, there was Mr Oliver and he always, always took to me, always, if there was any activities or, say for instance there was a year 5 was going on an activity and I was in year 6, right, it would only be a year 5 trip but I'd get an invite.
JB:	Ok. So why did you like him?
Horace:	(pause) because he weren't, he tried, he actually tried, to make a difference, he actually pulled his finger out and thought how's he gonna help . . .
JB:	And in secondary school?
Horace:	Secondary school, ah, my head of year, when I beat up that boy, Robert, I, I, my head of year come down and said "we need to have a chat". Miss Davies her name was, so I remember, remember

> the names, Miss Davies, she sat me down and said we need a chat. I said I know what you're on about the fight bla, bla, bla, bla, well I just said (inaudible) her, yeah I had to do that for these various reasons, as I, as I said it today it's karma with that and it's literally about five minutes after the fight. I weren't angry, I weren't "yeah I told him didn't I" I never done none of that, I just said, "well it had to be done", and she said she'd never, ever, ever, seen a kid, so calm, relaxed about violence, she said, she said, it's a good thing, because you're not angry, you're not, but then it's a bad thing because it isn't like you flipped and didn't know what you was doing, because you wasn't, you was calm. She said but, you're quite mature, because you never started kicking him when he was down, you've given him his whack, for what he needed and left it, you was a man who walked off, sort of thing, sort of, I reckon she liked me, from a weird thing really, but it was just how I dealt with the situation, I didn't start shouting and saying "No, I'm not in the wrong, I'm not in the wrong". I said, you know, I'm in wrong, shouldn't have done it, but I did (pause) so if you see what I'm saying, but after that, she sort of took to me, that's why, to be honest, I would have been kicked out, with me just running around the school, I beat up that kid, I was swearing at teachers and that, I should have been kicked out before I had a fight with the teacher, right, but because of Miss Davies, she kept me in, she put me on half a day, she done me a report card, whatever lesson I went into, I had to report. So, she kept me there as long as she, as long as she could literally drag it out.

In this narrative, Horace constructs the behaviours of Mr Oliver and Miss Davies in stark contrast to those of other boys. David and Andy constructed teachers as disciplinarians and judgemental, objecting to the "subordination" that Foucault (1977) argues is required within disciplinary regimes such as schools. However, Horace does not construct these two teachers in this way. Although both teachers were monitoring his behaviour, he did not object to their "gaze" but instead drew on discourses of caring and compassion to construct their observations as trying to help him rather than disciplining him. Earlier, parenting discourses were discussed, and in particular, how working-class discourses of behaviour are often considered at odds with middle-class discourses employed in schools. Earlier, Horace, drawing on middle-class discourses of parenting and childhood, indicated how parents should meet the needs of children. Likewise, it appears he also constructs Miss Davies through these middle-class discourses, understanding her as wishing to help him. This is in contrast to Horace's alignment of himself in working-class constructions of hegemonic masculinity.

Academic debates, while dismissing teachers as role models, argue that teachers' behaviours and disciplinary regimes have the potential to contribute towards the behavioural choices that boys make. This is significant in relation to Miss Davies's responses to Horace. Horace reported that Miss Davies did not criticise his fighting but instead praised his self-control. Using both a middle-class and working-class lens, Horace constructs fighting as not only wrong but also something he had to do. This self-appraisal appears to illustrate that while Horace constructs himself within a working-class discourse of dominant masculinity, through a middle-class lens, he also sees the limitations that such a construction has on his school life and education. Further to this, if, as Horace reports, Miss Davies did say to him that he was a "man" and was "calm" and "mature", this had the potential to mitigate his behaviour and reinforce Horace's construction of hegemonic masculinity by supporting the association of aggression with calmness, control, manliness and maturity. This resonates with Mills' (2001) "blueprint for normal masculinities" and the attributes and behaviours the "ideal man" displays.

Although Horace praises some teachers for being compassionate, ultimately their guidance does not help him because eventually he is permanently excluded from school. Horace's narrative illustrates the tensions not only operating between competing discourses but also how dominant discourses have the potential to prevail, resulting in the perpetuation of aggressive masculine behaviours constructed as disruptive in school.

In this next extract, Harry is not only complimentary about teachers and other adult help but also clear about what they should not do.

JB: . . . what do you think of the teachers in your school, in your previous schools, the ones you were excluded from, what were they like?

Harry: Um, there was a mixture, there was a lot of strict teachers but there was a lot of teachers you could talk to if you had a problem. But there were other teachers, they weren't teachers they were like people who were there for children with bad behaviour, who were always there to talk to, they were really kind but most teachers are really good at their job, but mainly didn't know how to speak to the children in the best way.

JB: Ok and what sort of things did they say that wasn't good?

Harry: I think raising your voice to a child who is usually naughty, is one of the worst things you can do, because the kid likes to assert authority, then he's obviously going to raise his voice back and he's going to get told off for it. I think if you talked to him calmly or her then they will talk calmly back to you and I think you have like a better relationship really. It will be easier to communicate, because if you shout and everything your gonna be shouting over each other trying to get the last word.

JB: Has that happened to you?

Harry: Yeah loads of times, when a teacher shouts at me I always shout back quick. I always seem to get on with the teachers that are more (um) (pause) quieter, not quiet, but don't shout at you because they are always understanding but even though they know something's wrong they will give you a telling off but they see it from your point of view as well not just they won't just, they won't just go down like one. . . . Will be like this is happening like, shout at you, they will explain things.

Harry begins this narrative by privileging a mentoring discourse to construct listening and guiding pupils as a necessary responsibility for teachers. He then, like Horace, uses a middle-class discourse of the "naughty" child, as discussed by Timimi (2005), to further construct some pupils as lacking and therefore needing adult correction, support and help. This appears to indicate that Harry acknowledges and accepts the hierarchical position of teachers in schools. It also seems to indicate that he accepts the "disciplinary regime" of school and the judgemental role of teachers who might "give you a telling off". While Harry's response looks submissive, it is not. Although Harry indicates that he may accept and yield to the authority of teachers, this acceptance and positioning of the school are done by drawing on a discourse of mutual respect between pupil and teacher. Therefore, he appears unwilling to be a submissive child but an adult on an equal footing. When Harry says, "the kid likes to assert authority, then he's obviously going to raise his voice back", he is indicating that this "kid" is unwilling to be submissive, as the teacher and the authoritative regime of the school prefer.

In the review of academic literature, consideration was given to the manner in which boys demonstrate and prove their masculinity to peers by challenging a teacher's authority. This may not be what Harry is discussing. Like John and Graham earlier in this section, Harry is drawing on a discourse of respect to construct some teachers' actions as discourteous. Unlike some other boys, Harry appears to accept his position within a hierarchical, disciplinary and judgemental school environment but only when constructed through his lens of fairness and respect. Therefore, when confronted with teachers who shout, Harry finds their attitude demeaning and aggressive and a challenge to his construction of himself within a hegemonic masculine discourse. Consequently, he shouts back.

Harry's comments and behaviour echo the beliefs and constructions made by several other boys interviewed. Bob, who was likewise critical of some teachers' attitudes towards pupils, also presented this topic when asked if he could remember anything about primary school.

> I can remember some of it, just normal stuff, just getting on, like, doing what you have to do really. But when I was younger I used to get on

> because you're scared of the teachers then, because if someone shouts at you then that's scary but like, obviously when I get a little bit older, someone shouting at me, I just laugh at them, so if someone shouts at me now, it's nothing, if someone raises their voice I can raise my voice back to them. But I could go one ahead and give them a slap for shouting at me.
>
> *(Bob, 16-year-old student)*

While echoing Harry's criticism of teachers who shout at pupils, Bob also illustrates how the relationship between pupil and teacher is actively reconstructed as boys grow and mature. In suggesting that younger pupils are scared of teachers, Bob is constructing primary schools not only as disciplinary and regulatory (Foucault 1977), but he is also objecting to the hierarchical structures in school. Drawing on a discourse of subordination, he constructs some teachers as controlling and dispassionate and argues that the obedience of primary pupils is achieved through fear determined by a pupil's age and immaturity. Applying a social construction of the child as immature and weak, Bob argues that with age, this changes; the child matures, and with this maturity comes enlightenment to the subordinating and disrespectful behaviour of some teachers.

This unfavourable construction of primary schools is formed through Bob's subjectivity within a discourse of hegemonic masculinity, a construction which demands performances of independence, strength and aggression. As such, the subordination that Bob claims exists in schools is in opposition to this, and confrontation therefore seems inevitable. In addition, boys' disruptive and aggressive behaviours are sometimes performed as a challenge not only to the authority of teachers but also to appeal to peers by showing how tough and independent the actor is. This was examined earlier, where boys discussed masculine behaviours and constructions of "showing off" in class.

In the boys' previous narratives, Bob and others express their unwillingness to accept disrespect from teachers or other boys. This sometimes resulted in aggressive confrontations. Being treated with respect, or as others put it, being treated as an adult male, was an expectation expressed by several boys. While Bob and Harry appear to be exploiting parallel discourses by demanding respect from teachers, there the similarity ends. Harry appears to be willing to comply with teachers' expectations as long as he is treated with respect, but in contrast, Bob may also use the opportunity for confrontation with teachers to "show off" to peers and thus further demonstrate his manliness.

In this chapter, I have so far examined a range of discourses, which potentially shape boys' choices and their behaviours towards teachers. However, it appears that the discourse of hegemonic masculinity remains dominant in shaping boys' behaviours in school, subduing alternative discourses and determining how they construct and implicate teachers in their behaviours. Foucault (1977, 1980) argued that control in institutions is achieved through surveillance and promotion of "normalising" discourses. While some boys seemed willing to accept the regulation and control of school, they did so only when this was accompanied by respect. Other boys were unwilling to relinquish their autonomy and constructed teachers as disrespectful, confrontational and unskilled in the management of bullying and peer disputes. Thus, for some boys, their relationships with school staff remain volatile and unpredictable. The relationship between boys and teachers remains the focus of the next section, in which teachers as role models will be considered.

Boys and teachers as role models

> you put someone in front of me with a suit trying to tell me that this is going to be your role model, I'll laugh at you.
>
> (Bob, 16-year-old student)

In the review of academic literature, I discussed the debate about employing more male teachers to act as role models to boys, which is constructed as problematic. In this section, I examine how boys variously responded to this idea. The boys interviewed in this study had all been excluded from school and thus had been variously constructed by schools as disaffected, aggressive and troublesome and therefore problematic. As such, these boys are among the pupils that policymakers regard as likely to benefit from having more male staff. I therefore considered it appropriate to seek their views on male staff as role models.

Merton's role model theory suggests that it is the character, class and behaviour of a person that contributes towards them being admired and copied (Merton 1957, 1986). In the following interview, it is possible to consider this construction by exploring how Harry explains what a role model is and whom he aspires to be like. Earlier, Harry and Horace appeared to merge parenting skills and the role model discourse, but when pressed, Harry was able to differentiate these. In developing his discussion about parental neglect, he defines his construction of a role model.

JB: Who do you aspire to be like?
Harry: Um, (pause) a sports person.
JB: Yeah, which one?
Harry: Hmmm, Cesc Fabregas . . . He's was an Arsenal mid fielder. . . . He's was just really good at what he does. (pause) it's not like (pause).
JB: When you leave school are you going to be a footballer then?
Harry: I'm not good enough to be a footballer, I would love to be a footballer, it's just one day, you dream about it.

Harry, although dismissing his own football skills, still constructs Fabregas as a role model. He states, "He was just really good at what he does", this signals that it may be Fabregas' expertise in his profession that inspires him to want to emulate an adult who is committed, talented, hard-working and the embodiment of sporting masculinity. Having dismissed his own football skills, the question is whether Harry can translate such commitment and ambition to an alternative career. As discussed, Mills warns that such "images of the 'ideal man' . . . forms the basis of hegemonic masculinities" (Mills 2001). Harry's construction of a role model may therefore do just this; by reflecting and embracing discourses of masculine fitness, strength and fame, he might be understood as embracing discourses of hegemonic masculinity. This in turn has the potential to reinforce gendered career aspirations and to resist and reject school, as Jackson (2002) argues.

Even though Harry considers that he cannot aspire to become a footballer like his role model, he is still vulnerable to the hegemonic masculine discourse that sports personalities and footballers embody. Thus, as Mills (2001) and others argue, Harry, like other teenagers, is vulnerable to popular media discourses and particularly peer discourses promoting dominant forms of masculinity as normal. These matters were discussed earlier.

As such, a boy's construction of the "ideal man" and therefore the "ideal" role model has implications for schools considering employing men for such a compensatory task. In addition, and as was shown in the previous section, a number of young male interviewees appeared to express their dislike, disapproval and distrust for some teachers. It seems doubtful that the character, class and behaviour of a disliked person would lead to them becoming part of a "reference group" and then being used by the young person as a model and for inspiration. How boys view the prospect of male teachers acting as role models will be the focus of the rest of this chapter.

David, a 16-year-old student, discussed at length his confrontational relationships with teachers. At the beginning of his interview, he was asked to recount his exclusions from school.

> And um, there was a teacher there, called Mr Brown init, and like, no one liked him init yeah, he was a proper arsehole like and that, and um one day he tried shouting at me yeah, I told him to shut up and then um, he goes, "Oh you insolent little child", and all this yeah, grabbed me from like the collar of my shirt yeah, picked me up yeah and I got mad yeah and started booting him yeah and told him (pause) punch shit and I got expelled for doing that.

David begins by saying that no one liked Mr Brown, and to give further credibility to his statement, he constructs him as "a proper arsehole", a stupid, irritating and contemptible person (OED 2014). David does not discuss what he had done prior to Mr Brown's actions. David is drawing on both a discourse of teacher competence and a discourse of children's rights to further construct Mr Brown's actions as unprofessional. David's narrative suggests that Mr Brown's behaviour, in shouting and grabbing him, may have been viewed by David as a challenge to his masculinity, thus provoking him to respond violently and physically. Although not selecting him as a role model, retrospectively, Mr Brown's aggressive behaviour has the potential to further reinforce David's alignment with dominant masculinity, thus illustrating, as Haywood and Mac-an-Ghaill state, "tough teachers make tough boys" (2003, p. 64).

As was shown in the previous section, many of the boys interviewed echoed David's expectations about the behaviour of teachers and their responsibilities towards them. With regard to the proposal that teachers might act as positive role models to boys, Bob, a 16-year-old student, had even clearer views about this.

JB: Right, now, I asked you about teachers now and this one is actually about that, the article says 'please sir we need more like you' they suggest that if there were more men teachers things would be better.

Bob: No, I don't agree with that, but see because in school yeah, like, it's different really like, in Princes like, I would work for Smithy because she was always smiling, always happy there was always a happy mood in the classroom and then, I would work for Sally because it's the same thing there's always a smiley thing, but then you got to Katharine's class, where I wouldn't work because she's a mood . . . well she's moody but basically like she just fucking, she just gets on our nerves, but then you got like people like (pause) Mike like, you would work for Mike cos he's always in a happy mood, say like you'd work for someone you had respect for, like Tim, he ain't always that bubbly and that but you'd work for him cos you had the respect for him. (pauses) Same as that would be for Bill or someone, you'd have the respect for them so you'd work for them, that's the same with John A [teacher] like (laughs) it weren't because his classroom was always bubbly it weren't cos you had the respect for him it was cos he was a funny bastard and you would just work for him anyway.

JB: Right ok.

Bob: And David always made his classes fun like but Katharine always just said well yes this is what you got to do, this is the explanation, do it. That was it, like you don't want that, like if that's the way, you gonna think well, this is boring, I'm gonna make it more fun, let's annoy the teacher (pause).

In this extract, I introduced a *Daily Telegraph* newspaper headline to Bob (Balchin 2006), which suggests that more male teachers would be helpful to boys. Bob dismisses this but instead draws on what appears to be a teacher competency discourse to construct the ambience teachers create in the classroom as a determinant of whether he will participate in lessons or not. This construction of a teacher's ability and skill appears to centre on their attitude, approachability and the enjoyability of the lesson. Bob also seems to place particular emphasis on humour, facilitating pupil–teacher relationships, which then determines whether he will respect the teacher or not. Bob's use of the term "respect" is different from previous constructions at 5.1 and 5.4, where boys demanded respect from teachers and other boys, expecting to be spoken to in a particular manner and treated equally and fairly as they constructed. While it was the policy of the Prince's school for pupils and teachers to use first names, Bob's use of the surname "Smithy" is a further indicator of his approval of this teacher and his construction of an enjoyable lesson.

Bob says that he "respects" teachers who are "funny, happy and bubbly". As such, he appears to be aligning himself with what are considered "laddish behaviours" as discussed, which are considered to account for some boys' disruptive and evasive behaviours in school. Further to this, the research of Barnes (2012) is relevant to an analysis of Bob's account. Barnes argues that some male teachers use forms of "laddishness", such as having a laugh, to get boys on their side and as a means of maintaining classroom order. This appears to be what Bob is seeking, receiving from some teachers and "respects". While this approach might appear harmless, male pupil and male teacher relationships constructed through "laddish behaviour" have the potential to reinforce rather than challenge discourses of dominant masculinity and, as a consequence, may perpetuate challenging and disruptive boys' behaviour.

Continuing his discussion about teachers making classes fun, Bob says:

Bob: But obviously, if the teachers like, making it fun you're gonna think, oh this is (laughs) a funny class, let's do what you gotta do.
JB: So the lessons need to be enjoyable?
Bob: Yeah.
JB: So it doesn't matter if it's a man or a woman?
Bob: Nah (pause) to be honest yeah, if it's a man I'm more likely to take the piss out of him in the classroom (pause) because it's a male but like females, I'm not gonna do that to because I have the respect to like, not to do that to a female.

Previously, Bob had affirmed his position within a dominant masculine discourse. He does this again when asked about his preference for a male or female teacher, saying that he would be more likely to "take the piss" and thus challenge a male teacher than a female because he has "respect" for females. In stating this, Bob is indicating how he is further drawing on discourses of gender binaries to construct female teachers as weaker and more vulnerable than men and therefore unable to withstand his ridiculing. However, a moment earlier, he had criticised the teacher Katharine for being moody and irritating and said that he might engage in disruptive behaviours to enliven the lesson and annoy her. This indicates that while Bob attempts to maintain a construction of himself within a "respectful" patriarchal working-class discourse of masculinity, his "laddish behaviours" have the propensity to undermine this.

In the final part of this interview with Bob, he is asked to reflect on another newspaper article that I show to him.

JB: This article here, this newspaper says, "Male teachers for role models", it suggests that boys need men as teachers because you will copy them, copy their behaviour.

Bob: No (laughs) no that ain't the way, you put someone in front of me with a suit trying to, err, tell me that this is going to be your role model, I'll laugh at you and tell you I'm not gonna dress like a stiff basically (Bob, 16 year old student).

Similar to other boys, Bob does not refer to social class by name but appears aware of the significance of the social class differences between himself and teachers. Thus, he laughs dismissively at the suggestion that male teachers would be a role model to him, seemingly identifying their dress as an indicator of social class. His use of the term "stiff" is not only used in reference to middle-class values and modes of dress but also suggests someone who is boring, inflexible and formal. Being in opposition to role models characterised by class asymmetries is illustrated when Bob retorts, "no that ain't the way", suggesting that the idea of the imposition of male role models is a simplistic and naïve solution to those boys' disengagement from schooling, which is a position supported by literature.

In the next interview extract, the issue of smoking and vaping in schools was raised. As was discussed in the literature review, some boys may rely upon their peers for guidance rather than their parents. As a result, some may engage in activities and behaviours, many of which are constructed as deviant by schools. Smoking may be considered one such activity. Milton et al. (2008) suggest that some young people associate smoking with their transition to adulthood. Therefore, some boys may view smoking as part of their transition into manhood. Dan discussed the relationship between smoking and teachers acting as role models. He begins by discussing being late for a lesson because he was finishing a cigarette.

Dan: Yeah but (pauses) look, in school, because, if one small thing happens and then you can't, in fact you might be late into lessons because you've been caught out of bounds and then you're all aggravated and you go into your teacher who say's one thing and that's it there's a row. But the teachers smell of smoke or they stand out and they're having a fag and they accuse people of smoking and they actually were smoking, just because they know you smoke.

JB: So teachers smoke but you are not allowed to?

Dan: Yes. And I'm (pauses) what it was, when I turned sixteen, you're sixteen, you're allowed to smoke, if your parents say you're allowed . . . (Dan, 16-year-old student).

Echoing the discussion covered earlier, Dan utilises narratives of freedom and independence to angrily object to the constant "scrutinising gaze" to which he is subjected in school. He considers this to limit his freedom of movement and restrict the choices he is able to make, one of which is smoking. He also constructs school policy as ambiguous and contradictory because teachers are allowed to smoke, but he is not. Thus, drawing on a discourse of equality and justice, he believes the pupil smoking ban to be unfair. Dan constructs himself as an adult free to make his own decisions and choices; therefore, like other boys in this study, Dan considers teachers' actions hypocritical and patronising because they construct him as a vulnerable child requiring the nurturing and control of adults. A teacher who smokes may appear rebellious and therefore appealing as a role model to teenage boys, but this is not the case for Dan. Instead, he disidentifies with these teachers because of the authority they have over him and, in particular, for what he constructs as their hypocrisy.

In this section, consideration was given to the recurring proposal that teachers might act as role models to boys. In the literature review, it was illustrated that much academic debate rejects the idea. In this research, boys also considered and rejected the idea. However, the notion that male teachers might act as role models to boys remains a powerful, taken-for-granted discourse taken up in policy and reinscribed in media debates.

Earlier, I discussed the views of male students and the part they considered teachers to play in exclusion. Drawing on a range of discourses, boys praised some teachers, but they also variously joked, ridiculed or expressed their dislike of other teachers, particularly those the boys located within discourses of disrespect. These teachers were considered confrontational, disciplinarians and subordinating. Excluded boys tend to frequently display behaviour to construct themselves within discourses of dominant masculinity. Acting in opposition to those in authority is a feature of this, particularly when confrontational behaviour is used as a demonstration of masculinity to peers. As such, it is therefore not surprising that research, such as that of Bricheno and Thornton (2007), confirms that few pupils consider teachers as role models.

Dismissal of and contempt for teachers challenges the hegemony of the "teacher as role model" discourse, particularly where teachers' age, class and masculine performances are considered incongruent to those valued by boys.

Summary

This chapter has explored how boys negotiate a range of complex and contradictory discourses as they manage the expectations of school, their behaviour, their peer group and particularly their constructions of masculinity. Analysing their narratives through a Foucauldian lens has made it possible to understand how some boys' constructions of truth and knowledge are informed by a mixture of discourses, miscellaneously validated by teachers, parents, media and predominantly by their peers. Foucault (1972) argues that powerful discourses create knowledge and ultimately truths. Discourses of masculinity described and discussed in the literature, and drawn upon and discussed in this chapter, provide a powerful illustration of the ways in which hegemonic ideas about gendered binaries, adult and child relations and class asymmetries become embedded within schools.

As the literature and this analysis show, male investment into the hegemonic masculine discourse affords it power and thus longevity. For boys in school, the strength of this discourse is furthered by peer pressure and self-policing. In their discussions, boys discussed and implicated a number of directly and indirectly related discourses in their constructions and understandings of themselves in school and their behaviour therein. These alternative discourses were subjected to scrutiny, but they were repeatedly marginalised as boys returned to the prevailing dominant discourse of masculinity for its apparent explanatory potential. It appears that investment in alternative discourses has the potential to destabilise boys' construction of a single normalised unitary masculinity, thus leaving them exposed and vulnerable to the likelihood of being constructed as childlike and non-masculine. For those "naughty" boys who have been excluded from school and therefore appear to be failing in school, this vulnerability is more acute, but this does not mean that other boys are immune to the influences of hegemonic masculinity. Peer pressure to adhere to hegemonic masculine behaviours affects all boys, and I would suggest that it has a lasting affect on all boys and men, at school and after.

What the analysis of boys' narratives has revealed is how the persuasiveness and pervasiveness of the hegemonic masculinity discourse make resisting it or contemplating accepting alternative discourses problematic. The analysis shows that some boys are drawing on a particular "regime of truth" (Foucault 1980) in their construction and normalisation of hegemonic, dominant discourses of masculinity, and this has the potential to limit their choices about their behaviour, relationships and ambitions and accounts for some boys' challenging behaviour and resistance to school. This also highlights that if taken-for-granted dominant masculine discourses continue to be left unquestioned, the normalising discourses that act to subjugate some boys will prevail and will continue to have implications for behaviours and attitudes in school.

In the next chapter, the narratives of school staff will be analysed to examine the discourses drawn on and to consider how their constructions align with, contradict or challenge the hegemonic masculine discourse and constructions of the boys interviewed.

Notes

1 It is clear from the whole of Bob's transcript that when he says people, "geeks and neeks", he is talking about boys. In other parts of his conversation, when referring to girls, he makes this distinction clear.

2 [NB: Horace was a very keen participant, being talkative and forthcoming. Horace introduced the discourse of role models without prompt.]

6

THE NARRATIVES OF SCHOOL STAFF

What will be examined in this chapter is how educational practitioners drew upon their professional and autobiographical experiences to make sense of boys' behaviour and exclusion. This chapter examines these narratives and will compare and contrast them with the explanations and experiences of the boys in the previous chapter.

Understanding dominant and aggressive male behaviours as normal

> it's inbreeded into boys, and they want to show off in front of girls and in front of other boys as well, I would think perhaps it goes back to, well, back to, probably back to hundreds and thousands of millions of years ago, when they wanted to, like I'm the man, I go out and I provide the food.
>
> (Dave, support staff)

Discussing exclusion figures, which indicate a disproportionately larger number of boys excluded than girls, Dave, a staff member in a secondary school, draws upon a similar normalising and popular discourse as some of the boys, suggesting that boys "show off" in front of other pupils to impress and demonstrate their masculinity. While some academic literature refutes the normalisation of these behaviours, it nevertheless agrees that they are performances designed to demonstrate manliness to peers. However, Dave further justifies and normalises his construction of such male behaviour by drawing on a "historical discourse", as discussed by Jablonka (2019) and Mills (2001), suggesting that such behaviours are instinctive, the result of "millions of years" of evolution. Similar to some boys' opinions, Dave also

DOI: 10.4324/9781003732785-7

seems to draw on a patriarchal discourse, "gendering work", as Haywood and Mac-an-Ghaill (2003) discuss, to normalise and construct men as the providers of food and security for their wives and children. This draws upon essentialist gender discourses, constructions that academic theory challenges.

Other educational practitioners used similar discourses to offer comparable accounts, echoing Dave's normalising construction of particular boys' behaviours. For example, Mick, a secondary school staff member, said:

> I get the impression that boys, we've had five thousand years of society where boys have been leaders and boys have got to be shown, they've got to show themselves, they see other men as being as like the leaders in society and they need to kind of do things to kind of emulate that and show they're kind of like in charge, I would guess. I mean, ok, these things have changed over the last ten years I suppose, but the girl kind of culture, because you often kind of often the girls, seem quite bad, but that is, the boy trying to be in charge of the situation I think it's kind of like the default setting.

In this narrative, Mick utilises four incongruent discourses. Firstly, and similar to Dave, he draws on a "historical discourse" to construct particular boys' behaviour as inherent and thus normal. He then contradicts this by adding that boys are "shown" and "see other men" behaving in a dominant manner. This explanation suggests that male behaviours are not innate but observed, imitated and learnt, and therefore, this aligns with academic explanations. This discourse therefore undermines the truth and normality Mick promotes in his first explanation. However, he follows this by suggesting that girls can also act "quite bad". This observation implies concepts of gender heteroglossia discussed earlier. Some boys also made comparable references. The concept of female aggression coexisting alongside male aggression undermines the often taken-for-granted assumption of the normality of male hegemonic masculinity by showing that aggression is not unique to men. However, having briefly introduced these two contradictions, Mick returns to a normalising discourse by drawing on a popular "truth", stating that boys' dominant behaviour is the "default setting". This further illustrates how the power afforded to this hegemonic masculine discourse has the potential to dominate contradictory and alternative explanations that might be used to describe and explain boys' problematic aggressive behaviours. The power afforded to this hegemonic masculine discourse is such that those subscribing to it struggle with the alternative and contradictory explanations that are available.

This is illustrated in the following: while constructing boys' hegemonic masculine behaviours as normal, some school staff paradoxically also criticised the behaviour, constructing it as damaging and destructive. Such criticism appears incongruent with constructions that accept this behaviour as normal.

This is illustrated in the next transcript, where Georgina, a secondary school teacher, begins by acknowledging the anguish that such boys' behaviour can bring about but then, like Dave and Mick, draws on a "historical discourse" to normalise boys' aggressive behaviour.

Georgina: but I just think boys' behaviour tends to be the brash (pause) physically violent and causing distress to others and to teachers and to other pupils and to teachers.

JB: I think a lot of people would agree with you, I'm just wondering why they behave like that.

Georgina: I don't know, I think we're going back to caveman aren't we? (pause) Back to role models, you know, girls' role models are people like, I was going to say Cheryl Cole but she is a really bad role model because she smacked someone round the face as quickly as anything (laughs), I think it's to do with socialisation, isn't it? (Georgina, secondary school teacher).

Having constructed boys' "brash" and "physically violent" behaviours as problematic, Georgina then attempts to normalise these behaviours by drawing on three alternative discourses. Firstly, she states, as Dave and Mick did, that such behaviours have their roots in prehistory; she pauses after this and then offers an example of role models, which she dismisses before finally suggesting, "it's to do with socialisation, isn't it?" Both the role model and socialisation discourse undermine the historical discourse by suggesting that masculinity is learnt and copied and therefore not innate. The role model discourse is itself not without anomalies and will be discussed further in the next section.

The apparent normality of violence and aggression among some boys was highlighted by Anne, a secondary school teacher. Discussing a school she had once worked in, she said:

> the lads, mmm it was predominantly violence, violence against members of staff and to a lesser extent violence against other pupils. Mmm there were incidents of knife attacks upon teachers, or thrashings and beating of teachers. . . . But violence is very much a currency and theme.
>
> *(Anne, secondary school teacher)*

Anne's statement was chilling in the manner in which she claimed such aggression and violence were perpetrated on fellow pupils and on school staff. Stating that violence was a "currency" suggests how entrenched such aggression was within this group of boys, illustrating how they were completely enveloped in a discourse of hegemony, which appeared so normalised as to have lasting effects upon them into their adult lives.

Anne also discusses how difficult it is for boys to resist peer influence. As boys acknowledge, and the review of literature shows, the peer group is very powerful, preventing and dictating some boys' behaviours and choices. Discussing this, Anne discussed a boy she had taught who wanted to read but had to first negotiate his peer group.

> this kid loved English, he loved English, but in his home he didn't have books, he didn't sit down and read, he couldn't be seen going into a library, you know, that was instant death. So this interest that he had was like a secret.
>
> *(Anne)*

As has been discussed, hegemonic masculinity is constructed in opposition to femininity; therefore, if reading is seen as a feminine activity, then we can understand how some boys might want to avoid it and how a peer group might respond with bullying and teasing to a boy wishing to engage in an activity that they consider abnormal.

It was shown in the boys' interviews that some boys also responded with claims about the normality of boys' aggressive behaviours, but some also recognised the influence of family and peers upon boys' behaviours, thus indicating (as Georgina does) that socialisation plays a part. As was discussed, academic research argues that boys' aggressive behaviours are learnt, thus challenging the normalisation of dominant masculinity and aggression and its supposed connection with "prehistory". However, the fragility of the historical discourse and the normality of male aggression are further destabilised by Georgina's reference to Cheryl Cole hitting "someone round the face". Such behaviour is another example of "gender heteroglossia" or female masculinity. While not referring to this, Georgina's dismissive laugh illustrates that she acknowledges the weakness in this argument.

The interview with Georgina indicates the fragility of the discourse that she, Dave and Mick and some boys draw on to normalise particular boys' behaviours. As has been discussed, male aggressive behaviours and masculine domination have been supported and justified through a range of discourses that grant superiority to males over females. While these three members of staff have unintentionally revealed the weakness of these arguments, by ignoring these weaknesses and subscribing to and accepting such dominant normative discourses, they may themselves be reinscribing narrow ideas about behaviours and subjectivities available to boys in school. This begs the question as to how things can change if school staff subscribe to the same problematic ideas about masculinity as the boys that they are supervising and teaching.

Male role models: responsible for, and a solution to, boys' behavioural difficulties

> there aren't enough men out there, there are too many women in teaching.
> (Grace, Education Advisor)

In this section, I shall examine how school staff variously discussed male role models as both a cause of and a solution to boys' behaviours constructed as problematic in school. The boys interviewed also referred to role models, arguing that parents and sportsmen both acted as such. Earlier, I argued that the role model discourse is frequently misinterpreted. However, featuring as it does in the media and endorsed by politicians, this discourse is deeply entrenched in debates about boys and schooling. It is therefore unsurprising that it was drawn upon so readily during interviews. But, while boys dismissed the idea of teachers as role models, educational practitioners did not.

Most of the educational practitioners interviewed drew upon popular discourses, which constructed particular boys' behaviours as problematic. They argued that problem behaviours were caused by a lack of "good" male role models and being subjected to "poor" role models. To combat this, some then drew upon discourses that advocated schools offering positive male role models to boys to address behavioural issues.

Grace, an education advisor, was shown newspaper articles advocating for more male teachers in schools. She responded by seemingly agreeing with the newspaper articles, drawing on media and government policy discourses, which argue that there are too many women in teaching and that there is a need for more men in schools to compensate. However, as the interview continues, her stance changes.

JB: . . . one says "Please sir we need more like you" and the other one say's "Male teachers for role models"

Grace: Yes there aren't enough, there aren't enough men out there, there are too many women in teaching (pause) (sigh).

JB: Do you think so? Why?

Grace: Well because I think, I think there aren't enough men out there being you know (pause)

JB: What sort of men would you like teaching?

Grace: (pause) just, I mean, I think, I actually, (pause) experience goes for a lot in teaching and you know, and an experienced teacher, you can't knock it, but there is something about young, vibrant teachers, that are really important, you know, all that old adage if you do, do, and if you can't teach or whatever but you know (pause)

JB: Yeah.

Grace: I don't know. (pause) I think there has to be a range of people and a range of sexes, a range of ages, a range of types, you know I don't go in with the fact that every teacher has to be fantastic, you know, not everyone is fantastic but you know I just think you have to have a range and I think you have to have a nice mix which reflects society really in terms of sex and you know and ethnicity and stuff . . . (Grace, Education Advisor)

Grace initially appears to readily agree with the newspaper headlines, saying that there are too many women and not enough men "out there". This indicates that she is drawing upon popular and powerful media discourses, discussed in the literature review, which construct female teachers as inadequate and a lack of male teachers in schools as responsible for boys' poor achievement and behaviour. However, she does not elaborate on this, and when pressed further, she hesitates and reappraises her thoughts. When Grace is asked directly what sort of male teachers she would approve of, she hesitates again before advocating something slightly different. Holding on to a role model discourse, she suggests experience, enthusiasm and youth matter more than the gender of a teacher. She then pauses again before explaining further that schools would benefit from a range of staff reflecting age, gender and ethnicity. What appears to have happened here is that, to begin with, Grace yields to the power of the popular discourse arguing for more male teachers in schools; however, when pressed to elaborate on her answer, she appears to realise the weakness of this discourse and so rejects it. She then seeks something more significant. Grace does not withdraw her statement that there are "too many" female teachers but draws on a variation of the role model discourse, arguing for a diverse teaching force, representing a range of age, race, ethnicity and class, so that school staff might reflect society as a whole.

Grace's initial acceptance of the male role model discourse and her subsequent hesitation and deliberation illustrate, as Foucault (1970, 1980) explained, that dominant and powerful discourses create knowledge from which people construct truths. It also illustrates that such discourses are difficult to contest or resist. Grace's change of mind may also show that she thinks that there may be an alternative to the male role model discourse. While popular media and government discourses appear to be dominant, academic literature on role models and boys' behaviour, as discussed in the literature review, is dismissive of the suggestion that male teachers provide a simple solution to the "problem" of boys' behaviour in schools. Cushman (2008) argues that schools should promote a range of male teachers and thus male behaviours; this reflects much of what Grace eventually advocates. Although Grace's new proposal unknowingly highlights the simplicity of the male role model discourse, what she eventually suggests is a diverse staff, which will promote an assortment of behaviours.

Other interviewees also commented on this issue, so I shall now examine four further examples where role model discourses were drawn upon. Dave, a secondary school staff member, commented in the same way as Grace did on the ratio of female and male teaching staff. As with some other interviews, his discussion was developed using newspaper headlines.

JB: What about this? [showing the newspaper cutting] There's "Please sir, we need more like you". What they are suggesting in another article too is that boys need male role models in school.

Dave: Yeah I agree with that, but then I'd have to (pause) because I'm male, but, but, I, I, noticed one thing, yeah?

JB: Mmm.

Dave: Um yeah, I would have to say that's one thing I was quite surprised about with the er, male minority of staff, be it teachers or supporting roles (inaudible) I'm in.

JB: Mmm.

Dave: Are, are in school, I was quite surprised with that actually.

JB: In what way do you think it would help then?

Dave: Um (pause) I think it would do, because they would look on . . . they're um . . . a lot of them do not see their father, not all of them, because some are out at work and all that and well I do work with, I do a lot of projects, once a week and when you turn round, one or two of them (pause) turn round and say to me, I don't talk to my dad like I talk to you or, and they done it to me a couple of times.

Like Grace's initial comments, Dave also refers to the ratio of male and female school staff, thus supporting popular discourse that advocates employing more male staff as compensatory role models. In doing so, he draws on the media moral panic discourse, which constructs the unemployed, single parents and absent fathers as feckless and inadequate and therefore responsible for the failings of their children in school. These constructions are similar to the parenting discourses raised by some boys in their critical discussions about parents and boys' behaviour in school.

In contrast to Grace and to Cushman (2008), Dave seems to be constructing men significantly, including himself, as having something to offer that female staff do not possess. As discussed in the review of literature, writers such as Mills et al. (2004) and (2008) argue that this belief is illogical and unsubstantiated. Although boys also rejected male teachers as role models, they contrarily used gender binary discourses to construct male attributes as different and superior to those of women.

Dave also stated that he had to agree with the proposal to employ more male staff because he is male. This appears to indicate that Dave so firmly constructs himself within a dominant masculine discourse that to say anything contrary to the newspaper proposals would, to him, be irrational and a challenge to his own construction of masculinity and gender binaries. If this is so, Dave's statement also indicates the fragility of these discourses, not least because his comments highlight the fear among males of not appearing masculine. When Dave says, "I have to because I'm male", this may show his recognition of the peer and cultural pressures upon him and other males to behave in a patriarchal, dominant, masculine manner. This obligation to perform is also reflected in boys' constructions of peer discourses in operation in schools and in particular their discussions about "showing off".

Writers such as Connell (1995, 2009) and the analysis of boys' narratives indicate the investment boys give and the power they afford to the dominant masculine discourse. Dave is illustrating much the same and in doing so is showing how the strength of this discourse is furthered by peer pressure and self-policing. For some boys, and it appears for some men like Dave, the dominant masculine discourse is so embedded within popular culture as to appear unquestionable.

At the end of Dave's comments about role models, he added that a few boys had said that they did not talk to their fathers like they did to him. I asked Dave to elaborate upon his understanding of what the boys were saying.

Dave: Perhaps because they don't, they don't have, like their dad, they say I never do this for my dad, or I never talk to my dad like this and it's really sort of thinking, have I achieved something here and to me personally, I have, you know, although, you know, a couple of times, they say, I wish you were my dad and that gets, like (pause) tear at the heart strings as well.

JB: Mmm.

Dave: Well I know some of them have only got or they (pause) you know, don't live with their dads or whatever, haven't got (pause) they don't have their father shall we say and it makes the job all worthwhile.

Here, Dave seems unsure of his opinions because he begins his response by saying "perhaps". His hesitant speech suggests that he is trying to make sense of the relationships and work he does with boys. However, similar to Horace and David's comments, Dave appears to be drawing upon a popular parenting discourse, where single mothers and absent fathers are constructed as feckless, and the role of a father figure is constructed as essential for boys. In doing this, he is further affirming the discourse of male teachers as role models. This affirmation was common among adult interviewees and is additionally illustrated in this interview with Michelle.

JB: Here's two articles, one says "Male teachers for role models" and "Please sir, we need more like you".
Michelle: Yes I think with some children, (pause) do make, some make really good role models and, and I know of children that are purposefully put in a male's class, especially primary school.
JB: Especially primary school?
Michelle: Yeah because they are missing their dads, isn't it? (pause) Or that they've never known their dad.

Michelle begins her answer saying, "Yes I think with some children", and then pauses. The break presumably refers to male staff but is omitted, perhaps because there is an assumption that the proposition is understood and accepted. She completes her explanation with a rhetorical question, applying a common parenting discourse to argue that male role models in schools will compensate for what she constructs as ineffective and/or absent fathers. Michelle's comments appear to illustrate, as debated in the literature review, that the strength of the male role model discourse is such that it is "embedded in our cultural common sense" (Clarke and Kitzinger, 2005), and therefore, Michelle considers that it requires little discussion.

In this final example, Simon, a secondary school teacher, discusses how his school utilised a range of adults, male and female, to work with disruptive boys at risk of being excluded.

> What we try to do is prove to them that they are worth something and most of these actually (inaudible) worth something to themselves. And staff that are here and they build a really good bond up with some of the staff, sometimes too close, um. Sometimes it's, you know, it's almost like an older person (sneezes) who is um unemployed, in their late sixties and who is like a grandma and she will give them a hug which I know is totally inappropriate and sit there, but it is, some kids lack that physical contact. We have another lady who is like an old fashioned mum who you know, checks they've had something to eat, make sure they, you know, everything's ok at home etcetera, etcetera. And we have quite a few male role models um, learning mentors who um, give them ideas i.e. most of our kids come from backgrounds where they haven't got two parents, most of them are single parent families um they have never had male role models and we try a lot of male role modelling i.e. um, that's, we talk about, how to treat women, how to treat their children, what their expectations be to their children and that sort of thing.
>
> *(Simon, secondary school teacher)*

In the analysis of boys' interviews, examples were given of boys who drew on discourses of neoliberalism to construct themselves as failures. Simon describes a similar group of disruptive boys in his school who also construct themselves as failures and therefore worthless. In defining these boys, and similar to other educational practitioners, Simon draws on a popular discourse, discussed earlier, which constructs the parenting skills of single mothers as inadequate and absent fathers as irresponsible. Of particular importance is Simon's statement that "they have never had male role models". This specifically constructs the blame and remedy within boys' understandings of themselves as men and their constructions of masculinity. Some boys drew on similar discourses to construct parenting and particularly fathers as essential and responsible for some boys' behaviours in school. While some academic research such as Clarke and Kitzinger (2005) and Donovan (2000) questions such discourse, others such as Herrenkohl et al. (2000) and Liabo and Richardson (2007) draw a similar conclusion as Simon.

While Simon's work tackling boys' difficult behaviours might appear admirable, it may also be problematic. Simon begins this extract by drawing on maternal discourses to describe and construct the work that female staff engage in with these troubled boys. He then draws on a patriarchal discourse to define the compensatory "role modelling" work that male staff undertake. By aligning the work of staff within these gendered discourses, this denies women the possibility of challenging boys' constructions of dominant masculinity and may contribute towards reaffirming the dominant patriarchal ideology of such essentialist discourses. Academic research and the observations of interviewed boys suggest that what are determined as masculine behaviours are not unique to men, but Simon's work has the potential to disprove this. As such, Simon's work is in opposition to that of Grace, at the beginning of this section, who dismissed the compensatory male role model discourse and instead advocated for a range of staff to work with boys.

These interviews with educational practitioners illustrate the power afforded to the male teacher role model discourse and how embedded this discourse remains in professional discourses. However, what Simon and other school staff appear to be advocating is not role modelling as defined by Merton (Merton 1957, 1986) but a discursive reconstruction. The incongruence of this popular male role model discourse potentially contributes towards its continued inappropriate endorsement. Grace advocated that schools should have a range of staff to reflect the age, gender and ethnicity of society. This would offer boys the opportunity to observe a range of alternative masculinities and would also be complementary to the discourses of mentoring and counselling approved of by some boys. Without this, schools are in danger of reinforcing discourses of hegemonic masculinity rather than challenging them.

School, parents and families

> they grow up in families, what do you expect?
>
> (Donald, therapist)

The interviews with boys drew tenuous links between parenting and role model discourses. In this previous section, some educational practitioners strongly advocated that male teachers as role models might compensate for "adverse" parenting. In this next section, I shall further explore respondents' constructions of parenting and their perceptions of the affects upon boys' behaviours leading to exclusion.

The discussions with educational practitioners, while often normalising displays of hegemonic masculinity, also criticised it and readily attributed unacceptable boys' behaviour to "poor" parenting. Some boys also drew on a parenting discourse, forming a link between the "quality" of parenting and boys' behaviour, which was constructed as problematic.

In the following interview, Andrew considers parenting and makes a similar construction.

> Machismo, yeah unfortunately most of the kids I come across where they're really ah, walked into the old macho, you know, behaving like a man unfortunately most of the time that is er, what they've seen in their role model, male role models. Often absent male role models for example, one poor boy, who must be about twenty now, that I worked with, he didn't have much contact with his dad at all, he knew his dad was in prison ror um, um GBH and you know, he very much put his dad on a pedestal in an effort really, to . . . you know.
>
> *(Andrew)*

Similar to some boys, Andrew draws a relationship among boys' behaviour, the parenting of the father and the adoption of hegemonic masculine values. He is also suggesting that the boy was anxious to have his father in his life (put his dad on a pedestal) despite the fact that he was in prison. Andrew's conclusion is that the influence of his jailed father was resultantly disruptive, as the boy valued "machismo", which he deduces disrupted his education. He adds:

> Machismo has nothing to do with actually taking in information of specifically, ah, being, you know, um social enemy, . . . the way with people round you is very much about them coming in and being very dominating and that's not very ah, conducive to learn.

Continuing to use the term "machismo", Andrew attempts to clarify how drawing on this particular masculine discourse disturbs education, disabling the ability to take in information. Somewhat confusingly, he adds that it is "very dominating", which is not "conducive" to learning.

In this next extract, without prompting, the therapist, Donald, introduces a conversation about what he considers bad behaviour, constructing a relationship between this and the affluence and prosperity of England compared with poorer areas of the world.

Donald: A lot of bad behaviour here is caused by a failure of people to realise how lucky they are. The forces of envy in England are if anything worse than anywhere else in the world.

JB: Why?

Donald: Greed and envy! Because appetite breeds disorder. There is excess but you want more. You're never satisfied with what you've got. This dynamic is very important both national and locally, I think with education too. In so thinking I'm lucky to have a school not to mention that I've so much food that I'm invariably fat nowadays. The doctors tell me off so that I complain that I've not got my needs met. I've not got the latest iPod, I've not got the special needs teaching, I never look that, I'm lucky to have a teacher period!

JB: But if you live in poverty, how does that view . . .

(Interrupts)

Donald: Well you live less long and so you got less time.

JB: But if you live in poverty in this country?

Donald: It's relative. That's my whole point and the differential is even greater in the third world. And that's how poverty is defined here. I haven't seen many starvers here.

JB: Because we don't allow people to starve?

Donald: Because there is over feeding.

JB: And people aren't hungry or cold or homeless?

Donald: And we tell people what their rights are. There is an arrogance based on a lack of appreciation of what one has, fuelled by greed and envy. There is an arrogant violence, which is rampant in England. It's one of the biggest taproots of the problem of bad behaviour in children and their relatives.

Throughout his rhetoric, Donald appears to reflect discourses of disapproval and the demonising of the unemployed as outlined by Cohen (2002), Jones (2011) and others. In doing so, he constructs the parenting of some adults as inadequate. This relates to the comments of the pupil Harry, who said that parents should inspire their children and set an example for them. Drawing on particular neoliberal discourses of parenting, Donald says that certain unemployed parents rely on the state and are lazy and greedy. Pupil

Horace spoke at length about his mother's partner being lazy and a poor example to him. Donald is also constructing such adults as uninspiring to children. Ignoring my questions about poverty, he draws further on an "inadequate" parenting discourse to further construct such parenting as contributing towards what he constructs as "bad behaviour in children and their relatives".

Throughout this narrative, Donald utilises a common media discourse, discussed by Jones (2011), constructing the working-class poor as selfish and ungrateful. As discussed, government data, such as Bowen et al. (2008) and Cotzias (2014), construct a relationship among poverty, boys' behaviour and exclusion from school. What these statistics do not highlight are the social inequalities linked with poverty, which are also considered potentially detrimental to parents and their children. Donald seemingly dismisses these matters. Drawing on discourses of greed, laziness and welfare dependence, he demonises some parents, constructing them as inadequate and ineffective, and therefore unable to be what he, and common discourses, construct as "good parents".

During his interview, Donald categorised all excluded boys into a single group, designated as "this mob". While condemning poor, unemployed parents for their lack of parenting skills, the use of this expression suggests that he is also condemning these boys for their inadequate school behaviour. Constructing both parents and boys at fault appears to be a contradiction, which is reflected in the following extract, where Donald is asked about the purpose of exclusion. In his response, he uses the expression "this mob" twice.

Donald: The purpose of exclusion is to drive this mob further down into a position where they will be even more tiresome and dangerous. So I think it's a very useful step to take on the way to damning them (pause) and they will take few down with them, won't they? It's a real get lost step, isn't it?
. . . interruption . . .

JB: What about their ability to have relationships with others?

Donald: They've got very good relationships with a lot of people this mob, actually but the fact that it's perverse is another issue. But they're very strongly bonded to society, they're thorn in its flesh. How closer can you get than under the skin of someone else? Isn't that wonderful? It's absolutely brilliant. They won't go away.

JB: And they choose this way of life?

Donald: Choice? They are driven rather than choosing.

JB: How are they driven?

Donald: By impulse. By instinct. It's that basic.

JB: So it's not choice? They don't have a choice?

Donald: Now we go into free will. That's philosophy but from a clinical point of view, these guys and some girls, they are on automatic pilot, there's a semblance of thinking and indeed discussion, is possible but any thinking or feeling is almost entirely self centred. So we are not having a dialogue here. We have not altruism or hardly any. They have very strong allegiances but that is dependent on having the same instincts. A herd instinct. They've a very strong peer group, the anti-socials.

As well as referring to these school pupils as "the mob", in Donald's final comments, he also refers to these boys as "the anti-socials". These comments appear to indicate that he draws on popular and media discourses to construct these pupils as slovenly and irresponsible.

When asked to define the purpose of exclusion, Donald draws on discourse, which constructs exclusion as derisory and detrimental, explaining that its purpose is to "drive" them (the excluded boys) further down. It appears, therefore, that Donald, while condemning parents and boys, is also expressing his disapproval of the sanction of exclusion. He then explains that the consequences of being excluded from school exacerbate an already poor situation and result in them "herding" together into a robust, self-reliant peer group, with no hope, prospects or empathy for others.

The views of Donald might be construed as somewhat disturbing and unhelpful in understanding how behaviours relating to hegemonic masculinity are understood and embraced in schools. However, his interview transcript serves to show the biases and prejudices that may exist within the school setting. Consideration has to be given to how such beliefs affect working practices and the behaviours of staff and boys in schools as a result.

In the literature review, the strength and importance of male peer groups were examined. In particular, it was discussed that hegemonic masculinity tends to dominate male peer groups, and within them, peer pressure is used to encourage boys to conform and participate in acts of dominant masculinity. Mills (2001) argues that this explains why violence features so prominently among certain groups of boys. Donald draws on parenting discourses to condemn certain parents and construct them as contributing to the behaviour of their children. This relates to academic research such as Lykken (2003), which argues that boys who have what are constructed as "poor" or "inadequate" parents are then more vulnerable to the influences of peer groups and perhaps to the "herding" to which Donald refers.

In one of my final questions to Donald, I asked him if he could account for the boys who construct themselves within a hegemonic masculine discourse. At this point, Donald makes a short statement: "Home is where it all begins, they grow up in families, what do you expect?" And then he paused, waiting for me to respond to him. While this statement might be construed as aggressive and dismissive, alternatively, it further confirms that Donald is drawing on common-sense, taken-for-granted parenting discourse to express his belief that home and family create behaviours, which are constructed as incompatible with school. However, rather than responding to his question, "what do you expect?", I ask Donald to explain why 80% of those excluded are boys. This led to a further development in Donald's reasoning:

Donald: Why? Because they are idiots.
JB: They are idiots because?
Donald: What you see is what you get. You see I think girls are more devious, it's a difference and it's there. Boys get caught more readily than girls, they're less smart. What I know is that, from a detection point of view, boys are less clever at concealment. That's my broad-brush impression. I think that male aggression is more striking, (pause) A metaphor. I think that girls are more poisonous . . .

As Donald had begun his answer by constructing "the home" as the cause of the boys' problem behaviour, there was an expectation that he might draw further on parenting discourses, but he does not. Instead, he draws on what appears to be an essentialist discourse of gender binaries, constructing a natural difference between boys and girls, with girls being described as "devious" and boys as physical, "idiots" and "less smart". Neuropsychologists, such as Baron-Cohen (2003) discussed earlier, use biological discourses in constructing and normalising differences in the behaviours and aptitudes of boys and girls. These discourses are in opposition to those of Connell (1995, 2009) and others who construct particular boys' behaviours as learnt. While the boys interviewed and discussed also appeared to draw upon an essentialist construction of gender, they did not define themselves as "idiots", although some considered that their behaviour had been foolish and had led to their failure at school.

In assessing boys' behaviour, Donald draws on a normalising discourse of school behaviour through which he compares and then constructs the behaviour of some boys as inappropriate. Foucault argues that behaviours that are considered to violate discourses of social norms may then be considered incomprehensible and therefore constructed as "mad". Although Donald does not quite construct these boys as "mad", referring to them as "idiots" demonstrates his and others' construction of these boys' behaviours as foolish, bewildering and incompatible with school. What is particularly striking is Donald's contemptuous dismissal of the young people that he is supposed to be helping, further illustrating how he blames them for their predicament.

Analysis of Donald's narrative has revealed that he draws on a range of differing and competing discourses to explore and explain boys' behaviours in school. These included blaming parents for their selfishness and ineffective parenting, blaming the boys for choosing to behave inappropriately and drawing on essentialist gender binaries to differentiate girls from boys and naturalise some boys' behaviours.

Earlier, I explored how the power of discourse shapes people's views and contributes towards constructing norms and defining truths. What will be shown next is how the discourses that Donald draws on, while seemingly incompatible and contradictory, reflect the views of other educational practitioners interviewed and therefore illustrate Foucault's contention that truth is endorsed and approved through discourse (Foucault 1970, 1980, 1982).

Johnny, an education advisor, was introduced to a newspaper article in which David Cameron had promised extra powers to head teachers to deal with troublesome pupils. Considering this, Johnny introduced a discussion about the influences of home life upon children. Similar to Donald, Johnny constructed the family home as the source and cause of the boys' difficulties. However, while Donald blamed parents for being greedy and lazy, here, Johnny appears more understanding of parents' difficulties.

Johnny: . . . Um, you see if you look at our authority and when it re-designated its special schools, seven, about seven, six years ago, it decided that there would be [1][a small number of] behaviour and learning schools of [between 80 and 120] children spread across the county, taking no account of the need in certain areas such as ours with a very strong, high level of deprivation, special need, unemployment, whatever.

JB: Does that affect it then?

Johnny: (pause) Well yes it does. There are greater number of special needs children in those areas and you see, and I was quite rightly told by an Ofsted inspector, that I was trying to point out the raw material, quiet rightly told to stop whinging and get on and the kids, the kids you know, they're the blank canvass that you can do what you will with them. You can't obliterate where they are coming from, you can't you know, you can't obliterate where they've come from in the morning and where they go home to afterwards.

JB: So why, what makes it more difficult for the unemployed and poverty and so on?

Johnny: Because a lot of them had um, (sigh) if people's spirits broken, it's very difficult to go on showing enthusiasm for something that, to engage in whole heartedly, perhaps you had a bad experience of education, that many of these people had, so you've got those coming back to haunt you. You've also got um the fact that your

> circumstances I think, don't, are not conducive to you being able to support your kids um on a daily basis. (Johnny, Local Education Advisor)

Drawing on discourses of deprivation, poverty and effective parenting, Johnny constructs being poor as disabling an adult's ability to parent their children adequately. These constructions concur with those of Katz et al. (2007) and others. Johnny also uses an SEN discourse to argue that special educational needs are more prevalent in areas of deprivation. This corresponds with UK government statistics, which draw a relationship among poverty, SEN and the number of exclusions. The relationship between exclusion and SEN is particularly relevant because some behaviours, constructed as incompatible with school, are contrarily constructed as special educational needs. Therefore, it is apparent that a number of the SEN pupils to whom Johnny is referring are pupils with behavioural difficulties.

After his confrontation with an Ofsted inspector, Johnny makes a particular construction of a child as a "blank canvass", at the will of an adult. This appears to position children within a Foucauldian hierarchical discourse where the child is the obedient, willing and "docile" novice (Foucault 1977). This is a discourse that several of the boys interviewed rejected and resisted, considering it disrespectful and a cause of confrontation. However, having formed this construction, Johnny abruptly employs a discourse of parenting, saying, "you can't obliterate" the influence of the home upon children. This sudden emotional statement suggests that Johnny is further constructing particular parents as contributing towards pupils' behaviours that are not conducive or compatible with school. Such a construction agrees with Donald's comments, some boys' observations and academic literature such as Lopez et al. (2008). However, Johnny then concludes that schools cannot compensate for or compete against the influences of deprivation or of such inadequate parenting. So, while Johnny has empathy and understanding for unemployed and poor parents, he also seems to be fatalistic about the prospects of schools helping these children.

Other practitioners also made observations about parents, in particular employing a parenting discourse to construct them as responsible for preparing and equipping their children for school. During discussions about what is constructed as disruptive boys' behaviour, Lucy, a teacher at a local secondary school, was asked how boys know how to behave in school.

> Well a lot of the time (pause) it can be choice that usually a child that from the cradle has witnessed how to make those choices, it's very difficult in the education um establishment (pause) with academic professionals that, let's face it, have put a lot of time and effort into their education and their

> qualifications to come into schools to pass that knowledge on, (Pause) and the child with the hidden disability, i.e. if mum gets out of hand, dad gives her a slap. So if my teacher tells me I've got to do something because if not I won't pass my exam, I might threaten, because this is how I've learnt to deal with the world. Um if siblings are allowed, (pause) out of control, I've found to abuse each other physically, verbally. When a child starts school, they present that behaviour to all the children around them because mother's never said stop, she's too busy playing online bingo or watching Jeremy Kyle, so as long as they're occupied. Okay?
>
> *(Lucy, secondary school teacher)*

At the beginning of this passage, Lucy employs a parenting discourse to argue that children construct their behaviour and the choices they make by drawing upon their experiences. While a child will have had experiences outside of the home, Lucy is referring to those in the family because she mentions experiences witnessed "from the cradle". Such a construction is similar to other educational practitioners and relates to academic literature where I discussed the discourse of parenting skills and how parents are variously constructed as competent or not. Lucy also makes a judgement about parents' daily activities, disapproving of particular television programmes and the playing of bingo, thus making use of a negligent, feckless parenting discourse to condemn and demonise working-class parents. At the beginning of this extract, Lucy's tone appeared to be suggesting an understanding of, and sympathy for, some pupils' behavioural "choices". But her sympathy then appears to shift to align with teachers instead, whom she constructs as professionals trying to do their job, which is hindered by certain pupils. However, using a disability discourse, Lucy now additionally constructs some boys' physical and verbally aggressive behaviour as a "hidden disability". This construction appears to support Johnny's comments, where he constructed those with behavioural problems as having a special educational need.

In her narrative, what Lucy appears to be doing is constructing two sets of victims. Firstly, she constructs those boys who have "hidden disabilities" as victims of inadequate parenting. Secondly, she also constructs teachers as victims unable to do their job properly and who suffer at the hands of their unruly, disruptive pupils. In constructing parenting as responsible, Lucy, like other educational practitioners, appears to be making broad assumptions, drawn from popular and media discourses about working-class families (Westwood 1996; Cohen 2002), to construct working-class parents as lazy, negligent and inadequate. A newspaper article by Frank Field[2] (2010) is an example of this discourse. The title of the article, "The biggest crisis facing Britain? Too many parents don't have a clue how to raise children", concisely reflects the constructions above.

While also constructing parents as responsible, in the following extract, Andrew, a therapist, offers a slightly different perspective on this matter. When asked how exclusion might be avoided, Andrew says:

> the main problem I see (pause) schools will tend not to address the issue and that's why we often get the um, the very difficult referral at the age of twelve or thirteen because the junior schools have tried to contain the child, as long as he doesn't go too over the top (pause) contain the child, until just before they get to secondary school. Then suddenly we start hearing about, you know, there's a boy who, you know, in school who might get referred to us, secondary, we might get the referral, my god and yeah, when you start going at that point, it's fire-fighting in its worse form, because by that time, the kid, you know, say twelve of thirteen, the child's had twelve to thirteen years of poor parenting, twelve of thirteen years of, you know, very, very poor role modelling, twelve to thirteen years of poor education.
>
> *(Andrew, therapist)*

Similar to Johnny, Andrew begins by using a compensatory education discourse but specifically to construct primary schools as negligent by not "addressing" problem children quickly enough. In Andrew's final comments, he also appears to resort to popular taken-for-granted discourses, saying that by the time he sees the child, they have been subjected to poor parenting, poor role models and poor education. In this respect, the blame that Andrew constructs is unlike that of other educational practitioners because it does not rest with parents alone. However, similar to Johnny, Andrew's comments appear to be without hope because he suggests that when the referrals arrive, it's too late and "it's fire-fighting in its worst form".

The varying comments of educational practitioners such as Donald, Johnny, Lucy and Andrew, while not completely unanimous, illustrate how discourses of parenting are readily employed to construct a parent's role as crucial in preparing a child for school. In particular, when things go "wrong", parents are then constructed as responsible for those behaviours that are considered incompatible or confrontational to school. As discussed, many of the discourses of parenting and behaviour relate to what are determined as middle-class values. This is further illustrated in the following narrative with Lucy, who introduced a discussion about discourses of good manners. Throughout Lucy's interview, she insisted that parents needed to prepare their children for school, concluding her argument by constructing some students as having an additional disability of having no etiquette because their parents had not taught them.

> A lot of students that come to us, they have no manners, it isn't their fault, they have never been taught. They've not been nurtured and

> polished by their nearest and dearest, they've been like weeds in the wind (pause).
>
> *(Lucy, secondary school teacher)*

Lucy's social construction of some pupils' etiquette as non-existent highlights the gulf between schools' middle-class values and those of the working classes. In blaming parents for not "polishing" children, Lucy is constructing their parenting as inadequate and their children as "weeds", failing because they have been left to their own resources. Her beliefs about good "manners" are founded on what she "accepts and makes function as true" (Foucault 1980). Similar to other educational practitioners, she uses particular authoritative and dominant discourses to construct "good" and "bad", with an assumption that these constructions, judgements and values are true and universally accepted. In doing so, Lucy, like other educational practitioners, is demonising alternative working-class forms of parenting and consequently condemning pupils who do not behave and perform within the discourses of normal behaviour that she employs.

Poverty and parenting

> I think that you never can believe that you can work your way out of poverty.
>
> (Anne, EBD teacher)

During discussions with educational practitioners, there were several unprompted references to poverty, with interviewees drawing a link among parenting skills, poverty and boys' behaviour at school. In the following section, I shall examine two representative views of educational practitioners.

Anne taught in an EDB school and specialised in working with boys who had been permanently excluded from mainstream schools. Discussing their various behaviours, she said:

> Poverty is such a, mmm, (pause) it overrides everything. If you live in poverty you get used to a certain standard of having to make do, and I think that you never can believe that you can work your way out of poverty. When they found out how much they could earn if they stayed on their mechanic course and became a mechanic they were really quite impressed with that, that they could make a living and make a very good living, out of it. Some of the poverty especially where we are down in [Eastshire], it's on the index of deprivation. These kids are not being fed, these kids are not being kept warm, some of the housing that these kids live in is questionable.
>
> *(Anne, EBD teacher)*

Anne initiates a conversation about poverty and then pauses, apparently in a melancholy manner, before she reflects and says that "it overrides everything". Her seemingly sad interjection emphasises the importance that she appears to place upon the impact of life with limited finances. Unlike other interviewees, such as Donald, Anne does not draw on discourses to construct the unemployed as lazy; instead, she suggests that the struggle to "make do" is all-consuming, such that people have little drive, ambition or belief in their ability to get out of poverty. Anne's comments appear similar to Johnny's explanation, which referred to people's broken spirits as disabling. So, while Anne might herself make use of a discourse of social migration, she indicates that the families and boys she worked with did not. Drawing on a common-sense discourse to construct education as a means of escape from poverty, Anne struggles to resolve why, when "they found out how much they could earn" as a mechanic, they could not engage in pursuing this career.

In the boys' interviews, some suggested that the aspirations passed on by some parents and families were uninspiring and lacked ambition. This comment is similar to the observations of Donald. While popular discourse such as that discussed by Jones (2011) and debated earlier has the potential to demonise and place blame on parents, Anne does not do any of this. Instead, she appears more sympathetic, arguing that the level of poverty that her students were subjected to was "on the index of deprivation", claiming they are deprived of adequate food, warmth and shelter. In making this statement, Anne appears to be reappraising the effects of being poor and seemingly reconciling the social inequalities that also affect those whose lives are overwhelmed by poverty to the point where they believe they can never "work their way out of poverty" and therefore acknowledge but reject the opportunity for social migration through education. This argument highlights how some boys' dissolution with school is such that it encourages their commitment to laddishness and problematic peer engagements, resulting in their alignment with the discourse of hegemonic masculinity.

Other respondents similarly constructed poverty as a factor harmful to male students. However, some did not thoroughly explain why they believed this to be so, with their responses appearing simplistic, with apparent assumptions that the discourses drawn on were universally accepted and understood. An example of this is provided by Olive, who at first discussed the complexities of educational failure and behavioural problems but then, when asked to expand her views, said:

> Poverty does feature, it really does, background features, partly because there is a, a lack, there's a lack of commitment to education with some parts of society and that is usually passed down to the children, so that they don't actually value education (pauses) and they don't want to participate in, it's a bit hard, they don't have to do it (pause). Some, some don't

get encouragement at home. Some have role model who are themselves anti establishment and that makes it very difficult for that child.

(Olive, local education advisor)

Olive begins by using a simplistic discourse to argue that poverty does "feature" in some boys' commitment to school. Having said this, and assuming it is understood, she swiftly appears to dismiss this discourse and instead draws upon an alternative discourse to construct society and culture, but particularly parenting, as responsible for boys' behaviour, under-achievement and distance from schools. In doing this, Olive appears to be utilising a popular media discourse to construct and pathologise poor working-class families as responsible for some boys' behaviours and disengagement in school. This abrupt U-turn aligns with the constructions of other educational practitioners and some boys who made comparable statements about parents' lack of investment in education.

In trying to understand the effects of poverty and make sense of some boys' behaviours in school, the dominance of particular blaming discourses is of concern. Not only does their employment ignore alternative and competing discourses, but it also leads to the strengthening of the construction of the working-class poor as lazy and unmotivated and their parenting as deficient. This further marginalises the social inequalities associated with poverty, particularly the relationship of poverty with under-achievement and educational disengagement, and therefore does little to tackle the issue of boys' aggression in schools or enable the development of any understanding of this matter. While the issue of poverty has merit, standing alone, it does not address patriarchy or discourses of hegemonic masculinity, which influence some boys, their peer groups and their reliance on aggression to resolve issues.

Special educational needs

well I think mental health, is one of the most underrated problems.

(Simon, secondary school teacher)

Previously, Johnny had mentioned SEN as a feature or cause of some boys' problematic behaviour in schools. Behaviour issues are constructed by some as special educational needs, so we shall now investigate this matter further. Foucault (1970, 1980) suggests that dominant discourses become the process by which truths are established. In the following section, this is demonstrated by Simon, who insists that mental health is real but "underrated" and consequently not fully appreciated or taken into consideration. In drawing on the powerful discourse of mental health, Simon offers schizophrenia as an example of the reality of mental health issues. Drawing on a Foucauldian perspective, Boyle (1990), considering schizophrenia, argues that mental health is socially constructed by comparing behaviours against and with "normal" behaviours. This is a useful analogy and will be used when considering the educational practitioners' views, which follow.

Above, Simon, a secondary school teacher, reflecting the opinions of other interviewees, appears to draw on a "mad" discourse when he determined that the mental health of some pupils was a significant contributor towards their aggression and inability to behave and engage in school activities. For Simon and other respondents, this occurs when behaviour is considered incompatible with the school's expectations and therefore outside of their constructions of "normal". Such a view relates to Foucault's analysis of the social construction of "madness". Simon argues that "mental health" is "most underrated". This appears to show that he considers that it is neglected as an explanation for some boys' violence and confrontational behaviour in school. He develops his argument further by giving an example of a boy who, he says, was later diagnosed as schizophrenic.

> Um, and when he came to us in year 7, he used to hear voices etc, and this has been, he has been like this every since he's five or six um he tried to set light to himself, tried to set light to a room um he, we, we, did the CAHMS referral, we had an emergency psychiatrist come over um, and that boy went through the next four years without a proper diagnosis and it's not until, (pause) because, in, you know, and what amazed me as well, many, many, many meetings about this young person and everybody agreed, "I think he's got schizophrenia". But because it can't be medically diagnosed until he's eighteen, you know, but everybody knew, but he wasn't going to treat him for it. He's now, you know, he now takes the drugs or whatever and he leads a fairly normal life but that young person went through hell for many years and I, it's that sort of thing, that always concerns me um and we, as um a school we always get um, I'm not saying we, we diagnose, I think that's wrong but we sometimes have a greater understanding of these young people, than sitting in front of a psychiatrist for a 20 minute session and sometimes kids can be, for want of a better word (pause) normal.
>
> *(Simon, secondary school teacher)*

Simon's dialogue illustrates the tension between school staff and CAHMS, arguing that CAHMS do not have sufficient time to assess a young person. In this respect, he constructs the "gaze" of the school as more effective than that of the psychiatrist. However, this assertion fails to take into account the varying discourses employed by institutions to construct "normal". It also fails to account for the possible incompatibility of these constructions between parties. Thus, CAHMS's construction of "normal" behaviour may not be the same as a school's, which in turn may conflict with the views of the boy being observed. Foucault insists that the behaviour of the "observed" is influenced by the "scrutinising gaze" of an establishment (Foucault 1977). While boys attending CAHMS might have been constructed as behaving cooperatively in school, some may have been oppositional to the hierarchical supervisory "gaze" therein.

In the discussions with boys, some discussed their objection to school hierarchy and the perpetual scrutinising gaze to which they were subjected, and this, they claimed, accounted for some of their aggression and behavioural difficulties. The influence of school upon pupils is considered further in the narrative that follows, in which Donald was asked to comment about psychiatric problems among schoolchildren.

JB: So is it possible that there are a number of children in schools who have psychiatric problems?

Donald: Yes. (pause) Often the school causes them.

JB: How?

Donald: Vicariously, through inadequate anti bullying policies. I'm not referring to the boys who will end up being excluded, I'm referring to people with deliberate self harm, and suicidal despair, caused by ill managed or badly managed bullying. So on from that point to yours it could be said that, roughly speaking, that the school has caused the bullying.

We also have the schools with the best intentions in the world, pushing them into excelling academically, and children feel valued in proportion to how well they comply with the ambition of the teachers, as you know, being a teacher yourself, it feels very good when your pupils have done well. So we get the academic exam time as now, with people getting in a panic over exam results, and they get a little bit psychiatric, so on that level you could say that education is bad for your health (laughs). But joking aside, this is not about boys being excluded this is a broader picture. There are, of the children being excluded, there is, at the retro-spectroscope, which is always a useful instrument, in cases that I've seen and cases that I've prevented/helped, where the exclusion is more or less predictable. When one considers the failure to secure a statutory assessment of special educational needs (pause) Complex children, with complex developmental delays, or failures or deficits, neurological deficits, pass below the radar, usually more so in Primary school, and sent to secondary school are absolutely not suited to the mainstream environment, and then progress, through bad behaviour, to the exit, they exclude themselves. Had they been statemented or had staff cottoned on to the fact that they had

> extremely unmet special needs, then the exclusion wouldn't occur would it? Because they would have been busy receiving, you know, a much more intense appropriate special needs package. (Donald, therapist)

In this extract, Donald makes use of a discourse of mental health in the same way as Simon to construct it as real. In addition, throughout this narrative, Donald also draws on a discourse of compensatory education to construct school as responsible for meeting a range of pupil needs beyond the academic. However, not only does Donald construct schools as responsible for meeting special educational needs, but he also argues that schools exacerbate or cause mental health problems in some boys. Such constructions are in contrast to Donald's earlier comments, where he stated that the home and parents were responsible for causing and creating problems. Some other educational practitioners, such as Lucy, did much the same.

Donald constructs two examples of mental health. His first involves his construction of the failure of school policies to prevent bullying and keep particularly vulnerable pupils safe, resulting in their "self-harm" and "suicidal despair". As was discussed, verbal and physical bullying is common among some boys and is principally used to enforce and demonstrate dominant masculine attributes. Earlier, attention was given to boys' constructions of bullying and peer pressure and how some boys considered this to contribute towards encouraging aggression and disruptive behaviour resulting in exclusion. As with Donald's previous contentions, a number of boys also discussed teachers' inaction, complaining that they did not intervene appropriately or quickly in pupils' conflicts. This appears to relate to Donald's assertion that schools "cause" problems by not having effective "anti-bullying policies". This also links to a discussion where three boys, Terry, Sid and Peter, argued that they were victims because teachers did not help them when they were being bullied. Like these three boys, Donald appears to be utilising a school policy discourse to argue that schools need to monitor and intervene in peer interactions.

In Donald's second example, he draws on a mental health and developmental discourse to construct the pressure of the school curriculum as damaging. He also suggests that some boys require additional support at school to compensate for their "complex developmental delays, or failures or neurological deficits". In saying this, Donald appears to be drawing on a developmental discourse to construct "normal" levels of achievement for pupils, which in turn are related to "target setting" in schools. Donald then appears to be arguing that what he constructs as "developmental delay" can be compensated for through additional school support. He further argues that a school's inaction and failure to meet a "special need" leads to violence, "bad behaviour" and exclusion. While it is evident that Donald is constructing the school as responsible, he is also determining how a boy's defensive and consequential retaliatory behaviour may be reconstructed as "bad" and result in exclusion. This was a view which was also variously constructed by some boys. However, what Donald's interpretations and judgements do not address is why a boy's reaction to school frustration, academic pressure and so on has to be responded to with violence or aggression. Donald's assessment seems to ignore the influences of peer pressure to respond in a particular fashion or if and how a boy is drawing on a particular masculine discourse in order to solve his frustrations with school.

In the following extract, in contrast to Donald, Andrew (who is a therapist working in schools) implicates parents in boys' disruptive school behaviours and mental health. Discussing boys who have been excluded from school and referred to his clinic for therapy, he says:

> The thing that saddens me most about an exclusion of a young person is, that, that's their record of thirteen and a half, fourteen, I think that is so damning of them and a lot of the time it's not, it's not that it's their fault, it's too much, it's too much at a young age. It would be different if they were sixteen and they were wilfully breaking, you know, all the rules, but thirteen and a half, fourteen? Their whole lives are chaotic, they've had poor parenting, they've had poor role models and they've ended up going to school, acting out on that limited poor input and that's it, then suddenly, you're the person that's permanently excluded, (pauses) and we've got you know, young people here who you know, are technically traumatized by the neglect of their parents.
>
> *(Andrew, therapist)*

In this extract, Andrew draws on a number of discourses to absolve 13- to 14-year-olds for their actions and instead positions parents as responsible. In doing so, he draws on discourses to construct these boys as vulnerable and with needs that should have been met by their parents. Because these needs have not been met, he determines that these boys are traumatised by what he constructs as neglect. This aligns with discourses of parenting and constructions of childhood, children's needs and parenting skills discussed earlier.

Some of the boys interviewed employed similar discourses. In particular, Horace discussed how his home life made him unable to focus at school, resulting in behaviour which led to his exclusion. Andrew uses a similar discourse to Horace, expressing an understanding of the trauma inflicted by "neglectful" parents and how such "poor parenting" can contribute to boys' behaviours, which may lead to exclusion. Drawing on these discourses, Andrew, like other interviewees, condemns particular parents as neglectful and unskilled.

Linked with parenting are constructions of childhood, which describe a child as lacking the competencies of the adult that they will become. It appears that these are conceptualisations that Andrew and others have taken up when they describe the needs of particular young people and the responsibilities of parents. Similar to Donald's earlier condemnations, Andrew describes "neglect" and subsequent "damage" that particular parents inflict upon their children. While Simon and Andrew medicalise particular boys' behaviour to construct them as problematic, they also construct particular parenting as a contributory cause of such behaviours. In this way, the discourse of parenting remains a powerful and dominant discourse in the discursive constructions of all interviewees.

This is further illustrated in the following interview with Thomas, who similarly utilises the dominant parenting discourse to attribute responsibility for boys' problematic behaviours but in doing so marginalises discourses of SEN and mental health.

> Going back to what I said earlier about parents we deal with, a lot of parents I deal with who don't want to take responsibility they always want to blame other people, I've listened to these same parents, say, uh, the reason why little Jimmy's naughty is, is cos, he's got ADHD or he's got Aspergers, oh yeah I get him some Ritalin, yeah, and it's the excuse of, there is a reason for it, it's nothing to do with how I've brought him up (pause) it's because there's a reason. But I think ADHD and illnesses like that should work across the social spectrum, however, it's only from personal experience, but a high proportion of children we deal with, with those diagnosis or more so with family thought processes, is they're still coming from the same areas, they're still coming from the high deprived areas, going back to what I said earlier, benefit dependency and social housing.
>
> *(Thomas, school behaviour manager)*

Although in this narrative Thomas draws on a discourse of social deprivation, he appears to disregard this in preference to a parenting discourse to construct parents as responsible for their sons' poor behaviours at school. Exploiting a popular media discourse, he refers to "these same parents", constructing a particular group who are feckless and irresponsible, wanting to "blame other people". Through his references to which Bupa explains as Attention deficit hyperactivity disorder, (Bupa 2009 and NHS 2025) and Asperger's, Thomas appears to construct mental health issues and special educational needs as real; however, he marginalises this when suggesting that some parents want their children diagnosed with a condition so as to alleviate themselves from blame. In doing this, Thomas appears to be classifying ADHD and Asperger's as social constructions. He is also further pathologising the poor working class while ignoring social inequalities linked with poverty. This illustrates how Thomas, like other educational practitioners, appears to rely on dominant popular discourses to seek understanding and solutions to his interaction with disaffected boys.

Unlike Thomas, other interviewees considered that some disruptive behaviour might be viewed as a special educational need. Where there were disagreements, these related to how interviewees drew upon other blaming discourses, with some interviewees prioritising matters that affected them the most. This is discussed in the narrative which follows:

> so where do you go from there? Well I put in Bill's name and I find that he has a statement and I find that his primary need is BESD, yes? And (pause) so it's about communication isn't it? And you've got three sets of kids and you've got three statemented kids but you're teaching four hundred and thirty two kids in all, so the other four hundred and twenty nine are the ones you kind of, I just think, I've hoped over the years that the profile of SEN will get moved upwards but I think whilst the onus [is] on heads to produce, produce academic results, the SEN kids will be overlooked.
>
> *(Johnny, local education advisor)*

Johnny creates a fictitious male pupil to discuss behavioural, emotional and social difficulties (BESD), which he constructs as a special educational need requiring the interventional expertise of a school. However, unlike Thomas and others, he does not undermine the reality of this special need but instead uses popular and academic discourses to discuss the implications and limitations of a school's ability to offer the help and assistance needed for particular SEN students. In doing so, Johnny acknowledges the popular discourse, which is used to construct such SEN pupils as unimportant and a waste of resources. He also highlights the pressure on headteachers to produce academic results, acknowledging that this has the potential to limit their willingness to prioritise resources to meet the needs of boys with BESD. So, while Johnny draws on discourse to validate BESD and therefore construct it as real, he also questions schools' ability to work effectively with these students, especially in light of academic priorities and accountability.

League tables and competition

> schools now devise ways of removing certain groups of the population who are not going to achieve that target.
>
> (Grace, local education advisor)

While some boys' aggressive behaviours were a notable issue for a number of interviewees, many also maintained that accountability, measured through target setting, Ofsted inspections and school league tables, influenced teachers' attitudes towards boys considered as disruptive. It can be determined that league tables are a form of competition among schools. Earlier, I explored the effects of competition in schools upon boys, illustrating how such competition discourages some boys from participating in school subjects in which they might not be successful. The question here is, do school inspections, league tables, competition and accountability also effect boys' behaviour and achievement?

Interviewees either introduced a discussion about accountability or were prompted to do so. Many argued that the various methods introduced to monitor and measure a school's success and effectiveness have had a secondary effect, limiting resources, discouraging patience and constructing intolerance towards boys who display disruptive behaviour. As discussed in the literature review, there exists an academic debate which draws similar conclusions. Above, Grace says that schools invent ways to remove pupils who cannot reach certain educational and behavioural standards. Being prompted to discuss this further, she said:

Grace: Targets generally, targets have um, a magical way of being reached and so therefore (laughs and pauses)
JB: (Laughs) What does that mean?
Grace: (pause) No, I mean obviously um, (pause) if you set a target, it's in everyone's interest to try and reach that target because (pause) not to get there in some sense (pause) is a failure with whatever repercussions that might have. So targets have a purpose.
JB: A good purpose, a useful purpose?
Grace: Yes, yes, yes, I do (laughs) think it sort of distorts you know what goes on, I mean if you have (pauses abruptly)
JB: How does it distort, tell me?
Grace: Um, well you know say for example you've got your minimum ninety per cent attendance target. (pauses)
JB: Mmm.
Grace: Well basically because if it's part of any kind of remunerative package (pause).
JB: Yes
Grace: Then resources will be put in ensuring that that target is reached.

Grace's opening statements indicate an apparent ambivalence towards targets. However, using a discourse of accountability, she then appears to accept the obligation of a school to meet targets because not doing so would indicate what she constructs as failure with consequences. While the work of Foucault (1977) may be used to describe the disciplinary gaze of the school over its pupils, now Grace is describing the scrutiny that the school is itself under and how this "sort of distorts". This suggests that Grace employs a particular discourse of education, the value and purpose of which have been challenged and reconstructed by accountability. This concurs with Ball (2003), who refers to this as "the audit culture", where teachers' values and beliefs are contested by government policy. Thus, Grace is aware of how targets have reconstructed the endeavour and focus of teachers and schools by redirecting the "gaze" on the school upon itself. As an example of this, Grace refers to attendance targets and how the resources of the school are repositioned to achieve this particular construction of success. While seemingly accepting this, Grace does not explain completely what purpose she perceives targets serve other than to avoid the punishment that failure would bring. She appears to be applying policy and media discourses to support target setting and accountability, but without revealing what value she attributes to the measures being set against her own discourse of education. Eventually, after further deliberating, I asked her:

JB: It's the repercussions of Ofsted inspections and target setting that concerns me.

Grace: Yes, yes, yes it's as (pauses abruptly)

JB: Does it impact on exclusion?

Grace: Oh yes, it impacts on (pause), absolutely (laughs). I mean yeah, no it really does.

JB: In what way?

Grace: Um, well (pause) I mean, we can just take a really simple target like A to C's percentages of A's to C's and schools now just sort of devise ways of removing certain groups of the population who are not going to achieve that target.

We had been discussing targets for some time, with Grace appearing to be vague, hesitant and somewhat reluctant with her responses. It is unclear why, but at this point, Grace looks to suddenly yield and declares, "absolutely", followed by "it really does". Possibly, my direct questioning influences Grace's answers, but her acknowledgement that targets can encourage the exclusion of particular pupils is given with a laugh, as if she is relieved to admit to this irregularity. It is also noteworthy that she does this as she moves the conversation from a simple Ofsted target about pupil attendance to a long-standing target regarding students' GCSE attainment. It is at this point that Grace declares that schools remove particular students who are likely to affect these targets. So, while using policy discourse to construct achieving targets as beneficial to schools, Grace also acknowledges that some students may be excluded in order to do so.

As was discussed in the literature review, the implications of Grace's comments are clear. She suggests that pupils whose behaviour is constructed as disruptive to their own learning and/or that of others may be excluded from school in order that the reputation and the academic and behavioural targets of the school are not compromised. If this is so, this is of concern because it is argued that boys who fail at school are more likely to engage in crime than those who complete their education (Reid 2005).

While Grace did not condemn target setting per se, other educational practitioners did, questioning the pressure and the subsequent effects that accountability placed upon schools and teachers. Simon, for example, referred to targets as "like this big axe that's hanging over teachers at schools. You know?" While Anne, who worked in an EBD school, which took excluded boys, argued that schools were scared of league tables and would exclude boys who were likely to interfere with examination results. Thus, both Anne and Simon appeared to be using a discourse of fear, as explained by Ball (2003), to explain teachers' responses to the policy of accountability. Explaining further, Anne said:

> I think the schools (pause) had become (pause) terrified of league tables because there were definite peaks when we would get students in and the closer you got to exams and the preparation of league tables, the more schools you'd get. The schools would just throw them out, and say you're excluded because you're violent.
>
> *(Anne, EBD teacher)*

Grace had suggested that failure to achieve a target had "repercussions". Anne is referring to these repercussions when she says schools are "terrified of league tables". However, her tone and language suggest that she is drawing on a discourse of social justice to disapprove of the actions of schools in excluding particular boys to improve the status of the school.

The social justice implications of this course of action are made clear by Michelle, an LEA advisor, who said, "they [teachers] are less tolerant with the children that cause problems, behaviour problems". Michelle explains that pupils constructed by the school as a "problem" were less likely to get attention and help than pupils who displayed behaviours which were compatible with the school ethos, showed educational potential and therefore might maintain or raise the status of the school. Such a view is particularly concerning. As one excluded boy said when asked if being excluded had helped him, he stated:

> No, No way, they never tried, never tried, helping me they just, realised I was a bit too, a bit too much to handle so they threw me away.
>
> *(Horace)*

This statement should be of huge concern to educationalists. However, while it appears that school staff understood the detrimental implications of accountability, they also seemed unable to combat them. Johnny, for example, discussing his experiences of working with boys considered near to exclusion, said:

Johnny: I am very, very quiet in front of newly trained teachers just because I hope they've got the idealism that maybe I did have, back in the late sixties, I mean I do have it now, I love working with these kids but I couldn't work with children now the way that I would want to work.

JB: Why?

Johnny: The trips that we used to take away, the freedom we had, the flexibility, you can't do those anymore.

JB: Why not?

Johnny: I don't really know what the answer is to that question, but (pauses and falls silent)

JB: What is it, the national curriculum?

Johnny: I used to take (pauses abruptly)

JB: Target setting or . . .
(Interrupts)

Johnny: That, that doesn't help within the classroom, certainly that doesn't help but I used to teach you know (pauses) I'm reading things about Jim's English is so poor, his literacy standard is so low, we've disapplied him from French or we've disapplied him from Spanish. I think that is so much rubbish. I did Shakespeare and modern languages with kids who've got very low reading ages, because you can do it in so many different ways in which you engage the kids, we had great fun and I don't think there is that flexibility, I don't think people have got the time.

Johnny is asked about the purpose of exclusion, but instead of answering this, he reminisces about when he taught "difficult boys". In doing this, he also appears to employ a discourse of social justice to implicate the current system of education and accountability in failing particular students by restricting the autonomy of teachers to match their needs. Johnny's objection is notably different from that of other interviewees. While he appears to argue that accountability restricts a teacher's time and the resources available to meet the needs of some pupils, in contrast to other educational practitioners such as Anne, Simon and Michelle, he considered it limiting a teacher's tolerance and enthusiasm to work with particular pupils. Nevertheless, both constructions have social justice implications. Using discourses of school status and accountability, educational practitioners' observations underline that pupils constructed as disruptive and non-compliant appear to be considered less valuable to a school than those constructed as compliant and achieving and therefore may be ignored, neglected or discarded.

Further discussion about the value of pupils was provided by Gail, a secondary school teacher. She begins her narrative by initially supporting accountability.

> Well I think there does need to be accountability, there does need to be recognition and a debate on what is it we want to educate our children to do. Um however, I think our focus has moved very much away, (pause) holistic development, from the whole individual, to achievement driven exam targets um and the two are not always compatible. We can have children who have tremendous abilities that aren't recognised within terms of exam success, however, there isn't for me in the system, the balance. I am not going to get as recognised by teachers in school for being brilliant at basketball as I am for coming out with five A stars, A to C including Maths and English, so therefore, that is always communicated, however we think we don't, we do, because it's a fact, at the end of the day that's what the teachers are looking for on their bits of paper. That's what they're judged by so therefore it cascades down.
>
> *(Gail, secondary school teacher)*

Gail's conversation begins by apparently seeing some merit in the current education policy of accountability; however, she then moves the conversation to evidently criticise it, seemingly questioning the policy discourse used to construct the curriculum and then that used to measure pupils' success. Her use of the term "holistic education" draws on a discourse of education, which values education beyond attainment and in addressing the needs of all children including problematic boys. This concurs with Johnny's comments and Simon, who had said, "what we should be turning out is, well rounded citizens for the country". Gail concludes that teachers' drive for examination results, "bits of paper", means that the focus in contemporary schooling is primarily academic, which inevitably further disadvantages the already disadvantaged, particularly working-class boys performing hegemonic masculinity. Discussing this further, Gail said:

> there are many merits in that, in terms of some quality assurance (laughs) for sure however, there is a deficit for the nature of the children that we are talking about, particularly boys because the benchmark of what is perceived to be achievement is not attainable to them so therefore, once they are able to know that and understand that, and I think if they do that at a relatively young age, there is no motivation, there is no point, because they are never going to be as valuable a commodity as the child who's going to get the higher A to C's. And I find it, although this is anonymous, that Every Child Matters agenda and that every child matters is fine, but in my

> experience, every child matters but it matters more if you're a D and we can get you to a C.
>
> *(Gail, secondary school teacher)*

In this commentary, Gail is torn between recognising the usefulness of the demands for accountability while also acknowledging the negative impact of academic failure on "particular boys" who cannot reach the "benchmark" of normality associated with targets. Like other interviewees, Gail constructs a unique group of boys who are disaffected and have behavioural issues. Not only does she have empathy for them, but she is also critical of policy rhetoric, illustrated by her final comments, when she paraphrases government policy discourse (DCSF 1995–2007; DfES 2004) and states, "every child matters", but it matters more if you can get good exam results. These comments further highlight how value may be attributed to certain pupils by schools.

While boys did not discuss target setting and accountability specifically, they indicated that they were aware of the discourses used in and by schools to construct success and failure. Indeed, both Horace and Bob used similar discourse to construct themselves as failures, citing their lack of achievement and qualifications as indicators. We know that boys who fail in education are far more likely to construct themselves within a hegemonic masculine discourse. Such a construction has the consequence of further distancing some boys from education by encouraging the adoption of aggression, risk-taking and other dominant problematic masculine behaviours, attributes which are ultimately destructive to the choices and discourses that these boys eventually draw upon.

Gail's emotive response reflected the responses of a number of practitioners. Many illustrated sympathy for boys constructed as having behavioural problems in school and variously acknowledged that, as a group, they had unique needs, which prevented them from accessing education. Some thought that these boys' needs should be addressed as a priority above academic interests; however, within the current educational framework, measured and assessed as it is, the value of these boys to schools is such that there are few resources available for them and therefore few choices available to help them. Subsequently, their future is likely to be both problematic and destructive to them and to society generally.

We know that competition in schools has the effect of disabling some boys from participating for fear of under-achieving or failing. However, competition in the form of league tables and school inspections also has consequences for some boys. By disabling some schools' willingness to put resources in place to deal with the complexities of their masculine behaviours, the subsequent repercussions of their expulsion from school may result in exacerbating their displays of hegemonic masculine behaviours.

Conclusion and summary

The analysis of the interviews with school staff illustrates Foucault's assertion that we create knowledge and truth through discourse (Foucault 1970, 1972). In exploring the range of discourses school staff drew upon, it has highlighted their vulnerability to the power and dominance of particular media and policy discourses, showing the influences upon their work, opinions and decision-making. Staff revealed the range of discourses drawn on as they look to manage and understand some boys. These discourses directly contribute towards their constructions of matters such as boys' behaviour, childhood and parenting skills while additionally influencing school staff's constructions of good and bad behaviour and where and how they apportion blame and responsibility.

Literature and the analysis of school staff's narratives show how they draw on and invest in discourses of hegemonic masculinity to construct particular masculine characteristics as natural and normal. This contributes towards the strength and perpetuation of this discourse and has the potential to contribute towards compromising the work that staff undertake with some boys. However, in their quest to understand behaviours constructed as incompatible with school, they draw on a range of other dominant discourses within which they search to normalise boys' behaviour and attainment and thus make judgements about right and wrong. These normalising discourses also contribute towards judgements about childhood, boys' behaviour, parenting and SEN. Respondents' narratives show these can have a profound affect upon the work and attitudes of school staff. While some constructions made are parallel with those of boys, others have the potential to antagonise and exacerbate problems.

Boys' understandings of masculinity and their engagement within discourses of dominant hegemonic masculinity are maintained and exacerbated in schools. While boys' understandings are influenced and encouraged by their achievement and/or failure at school and their interaction within their peer groups, it remains clear that school staff also have a highly significant role to play in this matter. The values and discourses that school staff draw upon are particularly important. I contend that if a school staff member draws upon a hegemonic masculine discourse or is in any other way related to or sympathetic with any dominant masculine discourse, then it seems incongruent for this staff member to be capable or suitable to work with disaffected, problematic boys. While we recognise that teachers cannot effectively work as role models to disaffected boys, it also seems logical that where school staff members draw on any discourse that promotes patriarchal discourses, their understandings, attitudes and abilities will be tainted and thus are likely to be ineffective if not counterproductive.

Notes

1 Numbers obscured to preserve anonymity.
2 [Frank Field is a well-known Labour Party politician who has been the Member of Parliament for Birkenhead since 1979. He was a director of the CPAG from 1969 to 1979. He writes for the pro-freedom of speech magazine *Standpoint*].

7

MALE SUICIDE

Within the assigned male characteristics of the "ideal man" is the requirement for men to be the breadwinner and home provider. Several of the people involved in discussions for this book referred to this expectation and responsibility. Earning a living and having a successful career/job appear to be crucial in defining this. While we understand that unemployment is difficult for both men and women, research argues that unemployment represents a particularly huge crisis for those men who align themselves with the "ideal man" ideology. The loss of their breadwinner status is especially destructive because it amputates a crucial portion of the masculine status to which they have pledged themselves (Willott and Griffin 1997).

At the beginning of this book, I suggested that an alien visitor would be intrigued by the destructive and problematic behaviours of men, behaviours that have the potential to cause significant damage. While many of the problematic behaviours of men harm others, many also harm men themselves. We are aware of prison statistics, road accident numbers and so on, all of which are dominated by men. What we have so far failed to look at is suicide and why it is significantly higher among men compared to women.

In 2015, the Samaritans' report on suicide statistics stated, "Across the UK, male suicide rates are consistently higher than females . . . the male suicide rate is approximately 3.5 times higher than the female rate" (Samaritans 2015). This appears to correlate with previously discussed statistics relating to men. The report also stated that "Suicide remains a major gender and social inequality". What I am about to explore is how much male suicide is directly related to the adoption of the "ideal man" ideology.

While one might think that male suicide has little to do with the problematic male behaviours I have discussed in this book, on the contrary, we

DOI: 10.4324/9781003732785-8

know that suicide is linked with the immense social pressures on men to perform and achieve. As many of the interviewees stated, performing as the "ideal man" is not just about being tough and aggressive; characteristics also include being the homebuilder, being the provider and achieving success. Many of the interviewees, both boys and school staff, criticised men who did not provide for their families. Academic research also highlights the negative effects on families of absent and ineffective fathers, with boys suffering when they do not have effective male role models or parental discipline (Donovan 2000; Cohen 2002). It is, though, important to note that much of this research relates to poor parenting, ineffective fathers and the absence of what is described as "good" parenting and a positive male role model (Liabo and Richardson 2007; Lopez et al. 2008). We understand and accept that men have a huge contribution to make to families and children. However, we have to recognise that the "ideal man" ideology places a disproportionately high emphasis on personal achievement, which includes the demand to provide for the family. This high demand has the potential to be very destructive.

In discussions about how boys are encouraged to adhere to outdated and stereotypical masculine behaviours, we have only briefly looked at men's emotions. In learning about how to be a man, boys also learn from peers and their family to suppress their emotions. Part of being the "ideal man" is to be strong and independent and not to show feelings. It is not uncommon for boys to be encouraged not to cry when hurt or upset (Askew and Ross 1988). It is also known that many men do not seek medical help when they need it or access medical help early enough when they have issues. And as for emotional help, many men suffer from restrictive emotionality because they believe it is a sign of weakness to discuss their emotions openly (Winnerman 2005). As a result, some men's physical medical conditions can go untreated, and significantly, their mental health can be put in jeopardy. Thus, it can be seen that by continuing to aspire to the "ideal man" ideology, a man's mental health may be compromised, a situation which can contribute towards suicide (Kennard 2020).

We also need to understand that a man's perception that he has failed may be exacerbated by his alignment with the "ideal man" ideology. We have already seen that competition and being successful are fundamental to the "ideal man". So not providing for a family may result in what is known as "Gender role conflict" (APA 2018). The question is what happens to men who fail in this regard?

This question is answered in part by an NHS report about male suicide, which suggests that the demands of the particular forms of masculinity contribute towards male suicide (Sutherland 2018). It is where men perceive that they have failed in achieving the high demands of manhood, such that their mental health can suffer, and suicide might prevail. Failing to provide for one's family is just one facet of these demands. This argument is further supported by a report from The Samaritans. It states that traditional male gender roles discourage emotional expression. Given that some men believe that opening up and discussing problems and emotions is a feminine attribute, this has the potential to exacerbate feelings of failure and shame. Men are told they need to be tough and that they should not need to ask for help. Thus, such rigid gender norms may make it difficult for men to reach out and ask for support when they need it. The report concludes that the perception of failing as a man is one of the chief reasons for male suicide.

In addition to this, the NHS report also maintains that there is something called the "gold standard" of masculinity. This, it says, puts undue pressure on men to perform and achieve. The report states that pressures on men include being successful, having power, adhering to competition and personal achievement, having control and possessing restrictive emotional behaviour (Donovan 2000; APA 2018). These personal values are much the same as those discussed through this book, which I have referred to as the "ideal man" ideology. Failing in any of these areas is problematic for some men. Some men believe that failure in life is measured by such things as being unable to maintain a secure income and attain and maintain a house and a comfortable family life.

Of further interest and importance is what the NHS report refers to as "The James Bond" style of masculinity (Sutherland 2018). This includes, as I have discussed, toughness, personal performance, physical size, fighting, independence, power and dominance. The NHS report argues that failing in these areas has wide implications for male mental health, and for some being unable to reach this standard, it may contribute towards suicide.

Similarly, a report by The Samaritans discusses how toxic messages about masculinity and how men should and should not behave and achieve can "eat away" at men's well-being. It is argued that the ideology of the "ideal man" is a prime example of such a toxic message, a message reinforced in schools and worsened by being accepted, adopted and promoted by the media, by peers and teachers and by the wider society.

Male suicide is not a sign of tough masculinity; instead, it could be argued that it is a sign that patriarchy has failed.

CONCLUSION, SUMMARY AND DISCUSSION

I began this piece of work to try to understand why so many boys were being considered "naughty" and, as such, were being excluded from schools. It has led me to understand that the root cause of boys' problematic behaviour in schools is also responsible for many of the issues which negatively affect men in their adult lives. The interesting thing about this matter is that the masculine behaviours, which cause these problems, are based upon an untruth. The media, society, families and schools draw upon a single but powerful masculine ideology, a discourse, which dictates that all men should be dominant, independent, impassive, competitive, aggressive, strong, clever and superior to women. While this ideology is based upon an untruth, in discussions with boys and school staff, all attempted to normalise such characteristics, even though they all appeared to understand the fragility of the discourse. This contradictory normalising of male aggression and risk-taking by school staff and boys was widespread.

While in schools, some boys attempted to resist engaging in problematic and confrontational behaviours, the power given to this particular form of masculinity makes it difficult to ignore and disables some boys from pursuing any other form of masculinity. The power afforded to peer pressure within boys' social groups is immense and is responsible for subjugating alternative views and constructions of masculinity. Thus, the consequential power afforded to masculine violence and aggression enables it, often via peer groups, to dominate, and in doing so, it also acquires normalisation.

When a young man leaves school, the pressures to adhere to the "ideal man" ideology do not disappear. While the confines of school might have exacerbated the power of peer pressure, the normalisation of the "ideal man" ideology remains within a boy after he has left school.

DOI: 10.4324/9781003732785-9

In film and TV, aggressive men are portrayed as desirable saviours (Miedzian 1992; Simpson 1994), while families and the media generally continue to support the power and normality of the "ideal man" ideology. Crime, including domestic abuse, does not alleviate in adulthood, and neither does the number of accidents caused by risk-taking. As mentioned, men dominate the prison population. While not all men engage in crime or risk-taking, the apparent acceptance of these high statistics is something that society takes for granted. Male behaviours, which cause these problems, appear ignored and normalised, possibly because these figures are, year in and year out, consistently high. It seems that society, passively, draws upon a discourse which presents and accepts masculinity in a particularly destructive fashion.

It does not have to be this way. If it were possible for boys to learn that aggression and violence were not a necessity, if they could accept and learn that so-called feminine interests and compassion and alternative forms of masculinity were acceptable, then we might be able to address the dreadful statistics of male destruction highlighted throughout this book. How this matter could be resolved involves a fundamental realignment of what society believes necessary and normal in twenty-first-century male behaviour.

It seems to me that if we want to reduce the damage that men are inflicting upon themselves and our society, we need to urgently find a solution to the issues of problematic male behaviour. However, before we can enter into any conversation about how we resolve this matter, we have to first accept and agree that a problem really does exist.

I have suggested that many of those I interviewed displayed aspects of "doublethink", that is, knowing and recognising that there is a problem, finding excuses to justify or explain away the issue and then refusing to accept that there is an issue after all. To effectively deal with matters that contribute towards men believing that they have to strive to achieve "ideal man" status, two things must happen. Firstly, it will be necessary for society, the media and families to take a good look and understand the damage that particular male behaviours are currently inflicting on our society. Secondly, they then need to accept the evidence, which shows such behaviour is unnecessary and avoidable. We must urgently look at how we all continue to normalise damaging hegemonic masculine attributes because, unless this is challenged, nothing will change.

It is blatantly evident that schools are an important and significant arena where boys are encouraged and coerced into drawing upon this hegemonic masculine discourse. It seems clear, therefore, that work could begin here in an effort to address the issue. However, the implication for schools is that school staff would themselves have to first refurbish their own understandings of men and masculinity if they are to engage in challenging and reconstructing boys' problem behaviours and related difficulties.

BIBLIOGRAPHY

Alba, B. (2019). If we reject gender discrimination in every other arena, why do we accept it in religion? *The Guardian*, London.

Allen, G. and L. Audickas (2018). *Knife crime in England and Wales*. London, H. O. Commons. http://www.parliament.uk/commons-library.

Allen, L. (2025). Hegemonic masculinity and addressing gender inequality. *The Journal of Men's Studies* 33(3).

Allen, V. (2020). Why men are twice as deadly at the wheel of their car than women. *Daily Mail*, London.

Anon (2024). French men urged to drive like a woman in new road safety campaign. *News24*.

APA (2018). *Guidelines for psychological practice with boys and men*. A. P. Association.

Archer, L., A. Halsall and H. Mendick (2005). *Dropping out and drifting away: An investigation of the factors affecting inner-city identities, aspirations and post-16 routes*. London, Commissioned by Esmee Fairbairn Foundation.

Archer, L. and H. Yamashita (2003). Theorising inner-city masculinities: Race, class, gender and education. *Gender and Education* 15(2): 115–132.

Arnold, C., J. Yeomans, S. Simpson and M. Solomon (2009). *Excluded from school: Complex discourses and psychological perspectives*. Sterling, Trentham Books.

Arnot, M., M. David and G. Weiner (1999). *Closing the gender gap: Postwar education and social change*. Oxford, Blackwell.

Arnot, M. and P. Miles (2005). A reconstruction of the gender agenda: The contradictory gender dimensions in New Labour's educational and economic policy. *Oxford Review of Education* 31(1): 173–189.

Askew, S. and C. Ross (1988). *Boys don't cry: Boys and sexism in education*. Milton Keynes, Open University Press.

Assarsson, L. and P. Aarsand (2011). 'How to be good': Media representations of parenting. *Studies in the Education of Adults* 43(1): 78–92.

Baines, E. (2024). Euros matches 'increase risk of domestic violence'. *BBC*. BBC.com.

Balchin, B. (2006). *Please sir, we need more like you*. London. http://www.telegraph.co.uk.

Ball, S. J. (2003). The teacher's soul and the terrors of performativity. *Journal of Education Policy* 18(2): 215–228.
Ball, S. J. (2006). Policy sociology and critical social research. In *Education policy and social class. The selected works of Stephen J. Ball.* S. J. Ball, ed. Abingdon Oxon, Routledge.
Ball, S. J. (2008). *The education debate.* Bristol, Policy Press.
Banner, J. (2015). *Exploring narratives of exclusion from school: How adolescent boys and educationalists negotiate schooling, family and gendered discourses.* Doctorate of Education, London Metropolitan University.
Barnes, C. (2012). It's no laughing matter . . . boys' humour and the performance of defensive masculinities in the classroom. *Journal of Gender Studies* 21(3): 239–251.
Baron-Cohen, S. (2003). *The essential difference.* London, Penguin.
BBC (2008). A fifth of teens carry a weapon. *BBC News.*
BBC.co.uk (2014). WW1: Why was women's football banned in 1921?
BBC.co.uk (2018). The truth about domestic abuse and The World Cup.
Benkinsella.org.uk (2025). Knife crime statistics.
Berger, P. and T. Luckman (1966). *The social construction of reality: A treatise in the sociology of knowledge.* London, Penguin Books.
Berman, G. (2009). *Prison population statistics.* London, House of Commons Library.
Bourdieu, P. (2001). *Masculine domination.* Cambridge/Oxford, Polity Press.
Bowen, E., M. E. Komy and J. Heron (2008). *Anti-social and other problem behaviour among young children: Patterns and associated child characteristics.* London, Home Office.
Boy, A. P. S. (2024). My fear at being forced into a state school by labour's new class war. *Daily Mail*, London.
Boyle, M. (1990). *Schizophrenia: A scientific delusion?* London, Routledge.
Bricheno, P. and M. Thornton (2007). Role model, hero or champion? Children's views concerning role models. *Education Research* 49(4): 383–396.
Brittan, A. (1989). *Masculinity and power.* Oxford, Blackwell.
Bupa. (2009). *Attention deficit hyperactivity disorder in children.* www.hcd2.bupa.co.uk.
Burr, V. (1995). *An introduction to social constructionism.* London, Routledge.
Butler, J. (1990). *Gender trouble.* London, Routledge.
Butler, J. (1993). *Bodies that matter: On discursive limits of sex.* Abingdon Oxon, Routledge.
Cannella, G. S. (1997). *Deconstructing early childhood education: Social justice and revolution.* New York, Peter Lang.
Carabine, J. (2001). Unmarried motherhood 1830–1990: A genealogical analysis. In *Discourse as data: A guide for analysis.* M. Wetherell, S. Taylor and S. J. Yates, eds. London, Sage.
Carrington, B., P. Tymms and C. Merrell (2008). Role models, school improvement and the 'gender gap'- do men bring out the best in boys and women the best in girls? *British Educational Research Journal* 34(3): 315–327.
Chambers, D., E. Tincknell and Joost. Van Loon (2004). Peer regulation of teenage sexual identities. *Gender & Education* 16: 397–415.
Clarke, V. and C. Kitzinger (2005). 'We're not living on planet lesbian': Constructions of male role models in debates about lesbian families. *Sexualities* 8(2): 137–152.
Cohen, A. K. and J. F. Short (1961). Crime and Juvenile delinquency. In *Contemporary social problems.* R. K. Merton and R. Nisbet, eds. New York, Harcourt Brace Jovanovich.
Cohen, S. (2002). *Folk devils and moral panics.* Abingdon Oxon, Routledge.

Coid, J. (2021). Epidemiology of knife carrying among young British men. *Social Psychiatry and Psychiatric Epidemiology* 56: 1555–1563.
Colman, I., J. Murray, R. A. Abbott, B. Maughan, D. Kuh, T. J. Croudace and P. B. Jones (2009). Outcomes of conduct problems in adolescence: 40 year follow-up of national cohort. *BMJ (Online)* 338.
Connell, R. W. (1995). *Masculinities*. Cambridge, Polity Press.
Connell, R. W. (2009). *Gender: In world perspective*. Cambridge, Polity Press.
Connell, R. W. and J. W. Messerschmidt (2005). Hegemonic masculinity: Rethinking the concept. *Gender & Society* 19(829).
Cotzias, E. (2014). *Permanent and fixed period exclusions in England: 2012 to 2013*. London, DfE, Crown.
Covington, M. (2000). Goal theory, motivation, and school achievement: An integrative review. *Annual Review of Psychology* 51: 171–200.
Covington, M. and K. Teel (1996). *Overcoming student failure*. Washington, American Psychological Association.
Crosnoe, R., C. Riegle-Crumb, K. Frank, S. Field and C. Muller (2008). Peer group contexts of girls' and boys' academic experiences. *Child Development* 79(1): 139–155.
Cushman, P. (2008). So what exactly do you want? What principals mean when they say 'male role model'. *Gender and Education* 20(2): 123–136.
DCSF (1995–2007). *Every child matters: Cross-government working with local partners to achieve better outcomes for children and young people*. London, Crown.
DCSF (2007a). *Confident, capable and creative: Supporting boys' achievements. (Guidance for practitioners in the early years foundation stage)*. London, DCSF.
DCSF (2007b). New exclusion figures show schools are getting tougher on bad behaviour. Retrieved 27/02/09. www.dcsf.gov.uk.
DCSF (2008). *The children's plan: Building brighter futures-summary*. London, DCSF.
DCSF (2009). *New exclusion figures show schools are getting tougher on bad behaviour*. News Centre: Department for Children, Schools and Families.
de Beauvoir, S. (1949). *The second sex*. London, Picador Classics.
Delgardo, R. and J. Stefancic (1995). Minority men, misery, and the marketplace of ideas. In *Constructing masculinity*. M. Berger, B. Wallis and S. Watson, eds. London, Routledge, 211–220.
DfE (2011). *GCSE and a level performance tables and school spend data*. London, DfE.
DfE (2014a). *Behaviour and discipline in schools: Advice for headteachers and school staff*. London, DfE, Crown.
DfE (2014b). *Permanent and fixed period exclusions in England: 2012 to 2013*. London, DfE, Crown.
DfE (2014c). *Provisional GCSE and equivalent results in England: 2013 to 2014*. London, DfE, Crown.
DfE (2019). *Permanent and fixed period exclusions in England: 2017 to 2018*. London, DfE.
DfE (2025). *Relationships. Education, relationships and sex education (RSE) and health education*. London, DfE.
DfEd (2018). *Permanent and fixed period exclusions in England: 206 to 2017*. London, DfE, Crown.
DfES (2004). *Every child matters: Change for children*. Nottingham, DfES.
Diamond, I. and L. Quinby (1988). *Feminism and Foucault*. Boston, USA, Northern University Press.
Doherty, B. (2017). *Hyper masculinity; influences and prevention in children*. M. College.

Donovan, C. (2000). Who needs a father? Negotiating biological fatherhood in British lesbian families using self-insemination. *Sexualities* 3(2): 149–164.
Doughty, S. (2013). One million children are growing up without a male role model. *Daily Mail*, London.
Elton (1989). *Discipline in schools (report of the committee of enquiry chaired by Lord Elton)*. London, Department of Education and Science and the Welsh Office.
English, O. (2021). *Fake history*. London, Welbeck.
Epstein, D., J. Elwood, V. Hey and J. Maw (1998). *Failing boys? Issues of gender and achievement*. Buckingham, Open University Press.
Epstein, D., M. Kehily, M. M. A. Ghaill and P. Redman (2001). Boys and girls come out to play: Making masculinities and femininities in school playgrounds. *Men and Masculinities* 4(2): 158–172.
ETSC (2015). Risk on the roads: A male problem? In *The role of gender in road safety*. G. Jost, ed. European Transport Safety Council. http://www.esc.eu.
Evans, T. and P. Wallace (2007). A prison within a prison? The masculinity narratives of male prisoners. *Men and Masculinities* 10(4): 484–507.
Festinger, L., H. W. Riecken and S. Schachter (1955). *When prophecy fails*. Minnesota, Pinter and Martin Ltd.
Field, F. (2010). The biggest crisis facing Britain? Too many parents don't have a clue how to raise children. *Daily Mail*, London.
Fine, C. (2010). *Delusions of gender: The real science behind sex differences*. London, Faber and Faber.
Ford, C. (2019). *Boys will be boys (power patriarchy and toxic masculinity)*. UK & US, Oneworld publications.
Foucault, M. (1970, December 2). The order of discourse (inaugural lecture at the College de France). In *Untying the text: A post-structuralist reader*. R. Young, ed. London, Routledge, 48–78.
Foucault, M. (1972). *Archaeology of knowledge*. London, Routledge.
Foucault, M. (1976). *The will to knowledge: The history of sexuality*, vol. 1. London, Penguin.
Foucault, M. (1977). *Discipline and punish: The birth of the prison*. London, Penguin.
Foucault, M. (1980). *Power and knowledge. Selected interviews and other writings 1972–1977*. New York, Vintage.
Foucault, M. (1982). The subject and power. *Critical Inquiry* 8(4): 777–795.
Francis, B. (1999). Lads, lasses and (New) labour: 14–16 year old students' responses to the 'laddish behaviour and boys underachievement' debate. *British Journal of Sociology of Education* 20(3): 355–371.
Francis, B. (2000). *Boys, girls and achievement. Addressing the classroom issues*. London, Routledge Falmer.
Francis, B. (2009). The role of the boffin as abject other in gendered performances of school achievement. *The Sociological Review* 57(4): 645–669.
Francis, B. (2010). Re/theorising gender: Female masculinity and male femininity in the classroom? *Gender and Education* 22(5): 477–490.
Francis, B. (2012). Gender monoglossia, gender heteroglossia: The potential of Bakhtin's work for re-conceptualising gender. *Journal of Gender Studies* 21(1): 1–15.
Francis, B. and C. Skelton (2001). Men teachers and the construction of heterosexual masculinity in the classroom. *Sex Education* 1(1): 9–21.
Funder, A. (2023). *Wifedom: Mrs Orwell's invisible life*. Penguin Viking.
Garfinkel, H. (2003). Socially negotiated knowledge. In *Social construction: A reader*. K. G. Mary Gergen, ed. London, Sage.
Gauntlett, D. (2008). *Media, gender and identity*. London, Routledge.

Gavita, O. A., M. R. Joyce and D. Daniel (2011). Cognitive behavioural parent programme for the treatment of child disruptive behavior. *Journal of Cognitive Psychotherapy* 25(4): 240–256.

Gee, J. P. (2011). *How to do discourse analysis*. Abingdon, Routledge.

Gergen, K. J. (2003). Knowledge as socially constructed. In *Social construction: A reader*. M. Gergen and K. Gergen, eds. London, Sage.

Gergen, M. and K. Gergen (2003). Constructing the person: Culture and critique. In *Social construction: A reader*. M. Gergen and K. Gergen, eds. London, Sage.

Gilbert, R. and P. Gilbert (1998). *Masculinity goes to School*. St Leonards, Allen and Unwin.

GOV.UK (2025). Misogynistic myths kicked out of classrooms to protect children. GuP release. *GOV.UK*. http://www.gov.uk/government/news/misogynistic.

Gove, M. (2011). *Michael Gove [speech] to the Durand Academy*. London. http://www.education.gov.uk.

Government, U. (2023). *Tackling misogyny in schools*. Hansard.

Green, G. (2007). Bullying: A concern for survival. *Education* 128(2): 333–336.

Gurian, M. (2001). *Boys and girls learn differently*. San Francisco, Jossey-Bass.

Gurian, M. and K. Stevens (2005). *The minds of boys. Saving our sons from falling behind in school and life*. San Francisco, Jossey-Bass.

Halberstam, J. (1998). *Female masculinity*. Durham, USA, Duke University Press.

Harari, Y. (2014). *Sapiens: A brief history of humankind*. London, Vintage.

Harris, A. and J. Goodall (2007). *Engaging parents in raising achievement. Do parents know they matter?* University of Warwick.

Havard, T. (2021). *Domestic abuse and Covid-19: A year into the pandemic*. London, H. O. Commons, Library, UK Parliament.

Hay, D. F., A. Payne and A. Chadwick (2004). Peer relations in childhood. *Journal of Child Psychology and Psychiatry* 45(1): 84–108.

Haywood, C. and M. Mac-an-Ghaill (2003). *Men and masculinities*. Buckingham, Open University Press.

Herrenkohl, T. I., E. Maguin, K. G. Hill, J. D. Hawkins, R. D. Abbott and R. F. Catalano (2000). Developmental risk factors for youth violence. *Journal of Adolescent Health* 26(3): 176–186.

Hess, L. E. (1995). Changing family patterns in western Europe: Opportunity and risk factors for adolescent development. In *Psychosocial disorders in young people. Time trends and their causes*. M. Rutter and D. J. Smith, eds. Chichester, John Wiley & sons.

Hewitt, J. P. (1976). *Self and society: A symbolic interactionist social psychology*. Boston, Allyn and Bacon.

Hey, V. and S. Bradford (2006). Re-engineering motherhood? Sure start in the community. *Contemporary Issues in Early Childhood* 7(1): 53–67.

Holland, J., C. Ramazanoglu and S. Sharp (1993). *Wimp or gladiator: Contradictions in acquiring masculine sexuality*. London, Tufnell.

Holton, G. (2004). Robert K. Merton. *Proceedings of the American Philosophical Society* 148(4): 506–517.

Hook, D. (2001). Discourse, knowledge, materiality, history: Foucault and discourse analysis. *Theory and Psychology* 11(4): 521–547.

http://www.prisonreformtrust.org.uk (2015). *Prison: The facts*. London, The Prison Reform Trust.

Jablonka, I. (2019). *A history of masculinity (from patriarchy to gender justice)*. UK, Penguin Books.

Jackson, C. (2002). 'Laddishness' as a self-worth protection strategy. *Gender & Education* 14(1): 37–51.

Jackson, C. (2003). Motives for laddishness at school: Fear of failure and fear of feminine. *British Educational Research Journal* 29(4): 583–598.

James, A. and A. James (2004). *Constructing childhood.* Basingstoke, Palgrave MacMillan.

Johnson, A. G. (1997). *The gender Knot: Unravelling our patriarchal legacy.* Philadelphia, Temple University Press.

Jones, D. (2003). The 'right kind of man'; the ambiguities of regendering the early years school environment – the case of England and Wales. *Early Child Development and Care* 173(6): 565–575.

Jones, K. (2003). *Education in Britain: 1944 to the present.* Cambridge, Polity Press.

Jones, O. (2011). *Chavs: The demonization of the working class.* London, Verso.

Jupp, V. and C. Norris (1993). Traditions in documentary analysis. In *Social research: Philosophy, politics and practice.* M. Hammersley, ed. London, Sage, 37–51.

Kane, J. (2011). *Social class, gender and exclusion from school.* Abingdon Oxon, Routledge.

Katz, I., J. Corlyon, V. L. Placa and S. Hunter (2007). *The relationship between parenting and poverty.* York, The Joseph Rowntree Foundation.

Kehily, M. and A. Nayak (1997). Lads and laughter: Humour and the production of heterosexual hierarchies. *Gender & Education* 9(1): 69–88.

Kendall, G. and G. Wickham (1999). *Using Foucault's methods.* London, Sage.

Kennard, J. (2020). Understanding suicide among men. *Verywell Mind.*

Knickmeyer, R., S. Baron-Cohen, P. Raggatt and K. Taylor (2005). Foetal testosterone, social relationships, and restricted interests in children. *Journal of Child Psychology and Psychiatry* 46(2): 198–210.

Kumudha, R. (2025, January 1). Study on challenges of peer influence among adolescents. *International Research Journal on Advanced Engineering* 3: 13–15.

Lareau, A. (2003). *Unequal childhoods: Class, race, and family life.* London, University of California.

Lauzen, M. M. (2023). It's a man's (celluloid) world (portrayals of female characters in the top grossing US films of 2023). womenintvfilm.sdsu.edu.

Lawler, S. (2008). *Identity: Social perspectives.* Cambridge, Polity Press.

Layard, R. and J. Dunn (2009). *A good childhood. Searching for values in a competitive age.* London, Penguin.

Liabo, K. and J. Richardson (2007). *Conduct disorder and offending behaviour in young people: Findings from research.* London, Jessica Kingsley.

Line, H. (2021). Tory MP: Men copying Kray 'role model'. *Daily Mail,* London, 5.

Lopez, E., S. Perez, G. Ochoa and D. Ruiz (2008). Adolescent aggression: Effects of gender and family and school environments. *Journal of Adolescence* 31: 433–450.

Lorber, J. (2005). *Breaking the bowls: Degendering and feminist change.* New York, W. W. Norton.

Ludden, D. (2020). Why do young men engage in risky behaviours. *Psychology Today.* Retrieved 30/10/21.

Lykken, D. T. (2003). The case for parental licensure. In *Psychopathy: Antisocial, criminal and violent behaviour.* T. Millon, E. Simonsen, M. Birket-Smith and R. D. Davis, eds. London, The Guildford Press, 122–143.

Macdonald, M. (2003). *Exploring media discourse.* London, Arnold.

MacNaughton, G. (2005). *Doing Foucault in early childhood studies: Applying post-structural ideas.* Abingdon, Routledge.

Manning, L. (2023). Metropolitan police expected to be heavily criticised for being racist, sexist and homophobic in report. www.bbc.co.uk.

Martino, W. (1995). *Gendered learning practices: Exploring the costs of hegemonic masculinity for girls and boys in schools.* Perth. Workshop paper presented at the "Promoting gender equity conference" Canberra, Australia. 22/24 February 1995.

Martino, W. (1999). 'Cool boys', 'party animals', 'squids' and 'poofters': Interrogating the dynamics and politics of adolescent masculinities in school. *British Journal of Sociology of Education* 20(2): 239–263.
Martino, W. and M. Pallotta-Chiarolli (2007). Schooling, normalisation, and gendered bodies: Adolescent boys' and girls' experiences of gender and schooling. In *International handbook of student experience in elementary and secondary school.* D. Thiessen and A. Cook-Sather, eds. Dordrecht, Netherlands, Springer, 347–374.
Mayer, G. R. (2001). Antisocial behaviour: Its causes and prevention within our schools. *Education and Treatment of Children* 24(4): 414–429.
Mayer, S. E. (1997). *What money can't buy. Family income and children's life chances.* MA, Harvard University.
McGrath, K. and M. Sinclair (2013). More male primary-school teachers? Social benefits for boys and girls. *Gender and Education* 25(5): 531–547.
McGuffey, C. S. and B. L. Rich (1999). Playing in the gender transgression zone: Race, class and hegemonic masculinity in middle childhood. *Gender and Society* 13(5): 608–627.
McLean, C. (1995). *The cost of masculinity: Placing men's pain in the context of male power. Promoting gender equity conference.* Canberra, Australia. Paper delivered 22/24 February 1995.
Merton, R. K. (1957). *The student-physician.* Harvard, Harvard University.
Merton, R. K. (1986). *On social structure and science.* Chicago, The University of Chicago.
Miedzian, M. (1992). *Boys will be boys: Breaking the link between masculinity and violence.* London, Virago.
Millham, S., R. Bullock and P. Cherrett (1975). *After Grace-teeth: A comparative study of the residential experience of boys in approved schools.* London, Chaucer.
Mills, M. (2001). *Challenging violence in schools: An issue of masculinities.* Buckingham, Open University Press.
Mills, M., M. Haase and E. Charlton (2008). Being the 'right' kind of male teacher: The disciplining of John. *Pedagogy, Culture and Society* 16(1): 71–84.
Mills, M. and A. Keddie (2010). Cultural reductionism and the media: Polarising discourses around schools, violence and masculinity in an age of terror. *Oxford Review of Education* 36(4): 427–444.
Mills, M., W. Martino and B. Lingard (2004). Attracting, recruiting and retaining male teachers: Policy issues in the male teacher debate. *British Journal of Sociology of Education* 25(3): 354–369.
Milton, B., L. Dughill, L. Porcellato and R. J. Springett (2008). 'Kids who smoke think they can be adults as well': Children's smoking and transitions to adulthood. *Children and Society* 22: 291–302.
Minogue, K. (2009). *To hell with niceness.* London, Social Affairs Unit Magazines. http://www.standpointmag.co.uk
Moalem, S. (2020). *The better half (on the genetic superiority of women).* UK, Penguin Random House.
Morrell, J. and L. Murray (2003). Parenting and the development of conduct disorder and hyperactive symptoms in childhood: A prospective longitudinal study from 2 month to 8 years. *Journal of Child Psychology and Psychiatry* 44(3): 489–508.
Mulligan, G., J. W. B. Douglas, W. A. Hammond and J. Tizard (1963). *Delinquency and the symptoms of maladjustment.* P. A. A. Moncrieff, ed. London, Section of Paediatrics.
Murlidhar, M. and S. Shastri (2016). Aggressive behaviour among elementary school children in Bangalore: A study on gender and grade differences. *The International Journal of Indian Psychology* 3(4).
NHS (2025). *ADHD in children and young people.* www.nhs.uk.
Nietzsche, F. (1913). *The genealogy of morals.* New York, Dover publications inc.

NSPCC (2012). *Legal definition of a child.* http://www.nspcc.org.uk/Inform/research/questions/definition_of_a_child.

OED (2014). *Oxford English dictionary.* http://www.oed.com.

ONS (2014). *Homicide index.* O. F. N. Statistics. http://www.ons.gov.uk.

Paechter, C. (2006a). Masculine femininities/feminine masculinities: Power, identities and gender. *Gender and Education* 18(3): 253–263.

Paechter, C. (2006b). Reconceptualizing the gendered body: Learning and constructing masculinities and femininities in school. *Gender and Education* 18(2): 121–135.

Paechter, C. (2007). *Being boys, being girls: Learning masculinities and femininities.* Maidenhead, Open University Press.

Parker, F. (2023). Starmer women problem' likened to anti-semitism. *The Daily Mail*, London.

Parliament, U. (2023). *Factors that increase young and novice driver crash risk.* U. Parliament. http://www.parliament.uk.

Pascoe, C. J. (2007). *Dude you're a fag.* USA, University of California Press.

Pattman, R. and M. J. Kehily (2004). *Doing research with children and young people.* London, Sage Publications.

Pattman, R., S. Frosh and A. Phoenix (1998). Lads, machos and others: Developing 'boy centered' research, *Journal of youth studies* 1: 125–142.

Paxman, J. (2021). *Black gold (the history of how coal made Britain).* London, William Collins.

Peal, R. (2014). *Progressively worse.* London, Civitas.

Pirrie, A., G. Macleod, M. A. Cullen and G. McCluskey (2009). *Where next for pupils excluded from special schools and pupil referral units?* London, DCSF.

Prado, C. G. (2000). *Starting with Foucault. An introduction to genealogy.* Oxford, Westview.

Reay, D. (2002). Shaun's story: Troubling discourses of white working-class masculinities. *Gender and Education* 14(3): 221–234.

Reeves, R. V. (2022). *Of boys and men (why the modern male is struggling, why it matters, and what to do about it).* UK, Swift Press.

Reid, K. (2005). The causes, views and traits of school absenteeism and truancy: An analytical review. *Research in Education* 74: 59–82.

Renold, E. (1997). All they've got on their brains is football. Sport, masculinity and the gendered practices of playground relations. *Sport Education and Society* 2(1): 5–23.

Renold, E. (2002). Presumed innocence: (Hetero)sexual, heterosexist and homophobic harassment among primary school girls and boys. *Childhood* 9(4): 415–434.

Ritchie, J. (1989). *Spare the rod.* Sydney, George Allen and Unwin.

Samaritans (2015). *Suicide statistics report 2015.* London, Samaritans.

Sax, L. (2005). *Why gender matters: What parents and teachers need to know about the emerging science of sex differences* New York, Broadway.

Scott, S., M. Doolan, C. Beckett, S. Harry, S. Cartwright and T. H. team (2010). *How is parenting style related to child antisocial behaviour? Preliminary findings from the help children achieve study.* London, Department for Education.

Searle, J. R. (1995). *The construction of social reality.* London, Penguin Books.

Shemilt, S. (2023). *Equity in cricket report.* BBC News. www.bbc.co.uk.

Sherriff, N. (2007). Peer group cultures and social identity: And integrated approach to understanding masculinities. *British Educational Research Journal* 33(3): 349–370.

Simpson, M. (1994). *Male impersonators.* London, Cassell.

Skelton, C. (2001). *Schooling the boys.* Buckingham, Open University Press.

Smart, B. (1983). On discipline and social regulation: A review of Foucault's genealogical analysis. In *The power to punish: Contemporary penalty and social analysis.* D. Garland and P. Young, eds. London, Heinemann Educational Books, 62–83.

Smith, D. J. (1995). Youth crime and conduct disorders: Trends, patterns and causal explanations. In *Psychosocial disorders in young people. Time trends and their disorders*. M. Rutter and D. J. Smith, eds. Chichester, John Wiley and sons.
Smith, D. J. (2004). *Parenting and delinquency at ages 12 to 15: The Edinburgh study of youth transitions and crime*, no. 3. Edinburgh, The University of Edinburgh.
Smith, D. J. (2007). 'Ye've got to 'ave balls to play this game sir!' Boys, peers and fears: The negative influence of school-based 'cultural accomplices' in constructing hegemonic masculinities. *Gender & Education* 19(2): 179–198.
Smith, P. K., D. Pepler and K. Rigby (2004). *Bullying in schools: How successful can interventions be?* Cambridge, Cambridge University.
Smith, S. L., M. Choueiti and K. Pieper (2014). *Gender bias without borders (an investigation of female characters in popular films across 11 countries)*. Geena Davis Institute on Gender in Media.
Staples, L. (2021). Why do men love spicy food so much? *GQ*.
Steer, A. (2005). *Learning behaviour: The report of the practitioners' group on school behaviour and discipline*. London, DfES.
Stern, M. (2025). *The execution of children and juveniles*. https://capitalpunishment.org.
Sutherland, R. (2018). Tackling the root causes of suicide. *EXPO 2021*.
Tapsfield, J. (2022). Boris says, "Putin wouldn't have invaded Ukraine if he was a woman". *Mail Online, Daily Mail*, London.
Taylor, S. (2001). Locating and conducting discourse analytic research. In *Discourse as data: A guide for analysis*. M. Wetherell, S. Taylor and S. J. Yates, eds. London, Sage, 5–48.
TDA. (2008). *Male teachers crucial as role models*. Retrieved 1/09. www.tda.gov.uk.
Thorne, B. (1993). *Gender play: Girls and boys in school*. Maidenhead, Open University Press.
Tilsen, J., D. Nylund and L. Grieves (2007). The gender binary: Theory and lived experience. *The International Journal of Narrative Therapy and Community Work* (3): 47–56.
Timimi, S. (2005). *Naughty boys: Anti-social behaviour, ADHD and the role of culture*. Basingstoke, Palgrave Macmillan.
Titus, J. J. (2004). Boy trouble: Rhetorical framing of boys' underachievement. *Discourse: Studies in the Cultural Politics of Education* 25(2): 145–169.
Transport, D. F. (2012). *Road accident statistics factsheet no. 1 – August 2012 reported accidents involving young car drivers: Great Britain 2011*. Department for Transport.
Traore, B. (2022). *Results of the first school climate and victimisation survey*. France, Ministere de l'Education Nationale.
Tyler, I. (2008). Chav mum Chav scum. *Feminist Media Studies* 8(1): 17–34.
UNICEF (2017). *A familiar face (violence in the lives of children and adolescents)*. New York, USA, UNICEF.
Uprichard, E. (2008). Children as 'being and becomings': Children, childhood and temporality. *Children and Society* 22: 303–313.
Vance, C. S. (1995). Social construction theory and sexuality. In *Constructing masculinity*. M. Berger, B. Wallis and S. Watson, eds. London, Routledge, 37–48.
Volman, M. and G. T. Dam (1998). Equal but different: Contradictions in the development of gender identity in the 1990's. *British Journal of Sociology of Education* 19(4): 529–545.
Westwood, S. (1996). 'Feckless fathers': Masculinities and the British state. In *Understanding masculinities*. M. Mac-an-Ghaill, ed. Buckingham, Open University Press.
Williams, B. (2020). *Thatcher, Margaret*. https://onlinelibrary.wiley.com.
Willis, P. (1978). *Learning to labour. How working class kids get working class jobs*. Aldershot, Ashgate.

Willott, S. and C. Griffin (1997). 'Wham Bam, am I a man?': Unemployed men talk about masculinities. *Feminism and Psychology* 7(1): 107–128.
Winnerman, L. (2005). Helping men to help themselves. *American Psychological Association* 36(7): 57.
Woodhead, M. (1997). Psychology and the cultural construction of children's needs. In *Constructing and reconstructing childhood: Contemporary issues in the sociological study of childhood*. A. James and A. Prout, eds. Abingdon, Oxon, Routledge, 63–84.
Woolcock, N. (2007). Ministers tell nurseries to allow boys toy guns. *Times*, London.

INDEX